Alan Ayckbourn

Confusions

Model Interpretations

by Albert-Reiner Glaap

Ernst Klett Schulbuchverlag

Acknowledgments

A. Ayckbourn, *Confusions – Five interlinked one-act Plays* is reprinted by permission of Margaret Ramsey Ltd, London.

J. A. Cuddon on *one-act* in: *A Dictionary of Literary Terms,* London 1977, by permission of André Deutsch Ltd., London.

Excerpts from pages 262 and 265 of *The Reader's Encyclopedia of World Drama,* edited by John Gassner and Edward Quinn. (Thomas Y. Crowell). Copyright © 1969 by Harper & Row, Publishers, Inc. By permission of the publisher.

Review of *Confusions* by Milton Shulman (Apollo Theatre) in the *Evening Standard,* 20 May, 1976. Reprinted by permission of London Express News and Feature Services.

Review of *Confusions* by John Barber (Apollo Theatre) in the *Daily Telegraph,* 20 May, 1976. Reprinted by permission of *The Daily Telegraph.*

The texts to which these interpretations refer are also available in a students' edition: *Confusions* (Klettbuch 5795).

Alan Ayckbourn's recorded version of *Confusions* is also available on cassette (Klettnummer 57957).

Gedruckt auf Eural PRO
hergestellt von Papeterie du Bourray
aus 100 % Altpapier.

1. Auflage 1 5 4 | 1996
Alle Drucke dieser Auflage können im Unterricht nebeneinander benutzt werden. Die letzte Zahl bezeichnet das Jahr dieses Druckes.

Umschlaggestaltung: Hans Lämmle, Stuttgart.
Druck: Gutmann + Co., Heilbronn. Printed in Germany.
ISBN 3-12-579530-3

Contents

Introduction

From the original five one-act plays, collectively entitled *Confusions,* three are included in the Students' Book. In an interview given especially for this edition, Alan Ayckbourn states that the three plays, in the chosen order, adequately reflect his original intention and retain the correct dramatic curve. The playlets can also be performed separately.

The Teacher's Book contains background information, study helps and practical suggestions. Since literary criticism is an open-ended, creative activity – especially in the theatre where no two productions are identical – no attempt has been made to give prefabricated answers. No recipes are given, nor even any detailed prescriptions. The "models" in the Teacher's Book offer guidelines and suggestions for introducing classroom work and discussion on some of the central aspects of the plays.

The background information and study helps centre around an interview with Alan Ayckbourn given in Scarborough on 26th March, 1981. The interview was "tailor-made" for this edition and can therefore be used directly in discussing the plays. Information on one-act plays and on the conventions of farce and comedy are also included together with some reviews.

Work on the text can be supported by using the Cassette, for which a few detailed suggestions are mentioned. In this section and in the section on property lists particular emphasis is placed on considering the performance of the plays on stage. The "Discussion Prompts" give examples of how a detailed study of either character, language or structure can be used as a starting point towards work on themes, topics and content. Relevant text references are quoted under the appropriate headings.

In the preparation of both Students' and Teacher's Book I have received valuable assistance from friends and colleagues. I should like to acknowledge my special indebtedness to Alan Ayckbourn who granted me the privilege of interviewing him on *Confusions.* My thanks are due to Ingrid Hartmann-Scheer and her students at Theodor-Heuss-Schule, Ratingen. There is much in the present book that I first learned from them. I am grateful to Joan Rafferty, who helped in the preparation of the manuscript, and to Gregory Fuller, of Ernst Klett Verlag Stuttgart, for many editorial suggestions. But my special thanks must be directed to Janice Probert who has been a friendly and resourceful working companion throughout.

Confusions – Five interlinked one-act Plays

Confusions is a quintuple bill, a collection of five mini-comedies linked by their similarity of theme. The playlets are about everyday habits, social duties, domestic embarrassments, human frailty and love. They deal with the difficulties that human beings encounter when trying to communicate with each other. The characters are British middle-class people in ordinary situations. "Nicholas! Stay in your own bed and leave Sarah alone" is the first line of the first play. A wife has been brainwashed by her maternal duties to such an extent that she treats even her neighbours with nursery discipline, just as if they were children. "Might as well talk to yourself" is the last sentence of the last play spoken by one of the five characters sitting on park benches where each is trying to make contact with the next.

The five plays are also linked by some characters from one play appearing in another. Lucy's husband, for example, who does not appear on the stage in *Mother Figure,* is the main character in the second play which is entitled *Drinking Companions.* Here he is a travelling salesman who tries to pick up two salesgirls in the bar of a provincial hotel. His attempts at persuading them to have a look at his hotel bedroom are in vain. He merely succeeds in getting himself drunk. The actor playing the part of the offstage husband in the first playlet appears again as the waiter in *Between Mouthfuls.* The deceived Mrs Pearce of this play turns up as Gordon Gosforth's local councillor in the fourth sketch called *Gosforth's Fête.*

Comments on this play and on *Drinking Companions* are contained in the interview with Alan Ayckbourn (p. 14; p. 15). As the dramatist has pointed out, the five plays can "of course be done individually, in pairs, in threes or whatever" (Students' Book, p. 6). But it would not be in line with his intention if the running order were rearranged, which has been suggested by some critics. Milton Shulman, to mention but one, claims in his review of the play that the dramatist should "switch the order of his final two plays and send the audience rollicking with laughter into Shaftesbury Avenue" (p. 23). To Ayckbourn *A Talk in the Park* is like a fugue and should therefore be the very last in order. Accordingly the three plays *Mother Figure, Between Mouthfuls* and *A Talk in the Park* should be read and discussed in the order in which they appear in the Students' Book.

Background Information

One-Act or Short Play

J. A. Cuddon in *A Dictionary of Literary Terms* (London: Deutsch 1977, pp. 455–456) defines the one-act play as follows:

one-act play Self-evidently a dramatic work consisting of only one act. Usually short (a playing time of fifteen to forty minutes is about normal). Very rare before late in the 19th c. though there are many earlier examples of shortish plays which could qualify as one-act plays, and the after-piece popular in the 18th c., was a kind of one-act play. However, towards the end of the 19th c. an increasing number of small experimental theatres greatly encouraged the development of the one-act drama as a form in its own right and it was often used as a curtain-raiser. Since that period it has flourished and is as popular as ever, though seldom used as a curtain-raiser. A more common practice now is to present two or three one-act plays by way of a double or triple bill. Two recent examples of this are Harold Pinter's *Landscape and Silence* (1970) and John Mortimer's *Come As You Are* (1971).

A one-act play is the dramatic equivalent of a short story and tends to concentrate on a single episode or situation and as a general rule has only two or three characters. In theme, mood and subject the range is considerable – from farce to tragedy. Many famous dramatists have attempted the form, including Chekhov, Strindberg, Shaw, Hauptmann, Synge, J. M. Barrie, Eugene O'Neill, Samuel Beckett and Harold Pinter.

As Alan Ayckbourn points out, the five plays of *Confusions*, although they form one whole, can be dealt with and produced separately because each of them is a self-contained unit. Literary critics even tend to drop the term *one-act play* altogether and replace it by *short play* which, in their opinion, expresses in a much better way what is characteristic of this type of play. Indeed, as regards structure and portrayal of characters, *short play* is a more appropriate word. For brevity is as much a characteristic feature of this genre as it is of the short story. Moreover the word "act" in *one-act play* is misleading in as far as it suggests that the play is only part of a more comprehensive drama.

In two articles, Heinz Kosok (1965 and 1970) summarizes and explains the characteristic elements of the *short play*, the most important of which are:

- conciseness and brevity,
- unity of time and place,
- absence of subplots,
- emphasis on situation rather than on plot,
- concentration on critical situations,
- small number of characters,
- presentation of characters reduced to portrayal of their most striking traits,
- succinct dialogues.

In the nineteenth century a sort of short play often served the function of a *curtain-raiser*. It used to be performed before the actual full-length play started, thus catering for both "the early birds" and the late-comers in the audience. Under the influence of the repertory theatre movement (e.g. Abbey Theatre in Dublin) at the turn of this century what are short plays in our modern understanding came into being. Most of them were played as *triple bills:* three plays were staged in the course of one evening, thus presenting the audience with a kaleidoscope of characters and a wide technical variety.

Short plays are suitable material for literature classes just as much as short stories. Both require that the students concentrate at once on essential elements of structure and characterization. There is no time to deal with preliminaries or account for the function of the exposition because there is none. The short play "gets down to brass tacks" without any delay.

Comedy and Farce

farce. One of the principal classifications of the nonmusical drama, the others being tragedy, melodrama, and comedy. Farce is sometimes confused with broad comedy; the two may be separated in theory by saying that farce draws its humor from physical activity on stage arising from the given situation, whereas comedy depends on the study of characters and the attempts by these characters to be witty. The appeal of farce is therefore primarily visual and sensuous; that of comedy, auditory and intellectual. Even so, plays that are labeled or recognized as farces may steal scenes or moments from comedy, while comedy may incorporate bits of business—*lazzi* or, as they are called on Broadway, "shticks"—that are clearly farcical. In practice, especially in performance, the division is not a hard-and-fast one. Nor are there, in the history of the theater, many examples of plays that are farcical throughout ...

To achieve the desired unreality of mood and to court the desired response, laughter, the playwright will generally begin his farce in commonplace, credible circumstances and surroundings. Then by means of theatrical logic he will shift it gradually into improbability and beyond that into the realm of nonsense. (In contemporary farce the progression tends to be more abrupt, while logic has given way to a blatant use of "antilogic".) By bringing in a string of fresh complications, by uncovering secrets and letting out surprising revelations, by the introduction of coincidences and accidents, he does not give his audience a chance to see quite how the action is developing, nor to find a psychological footing, until his plot maneuvers have entrapped his characters. The cast is in continual flux with new arrivals and sudden departures. The precipitous entrance and exit are the most common stage directions in farce. They enhance the instability of the action; they intensify the bustle; they foster a feeling in the onlookers of uncertainty. Anything can happen next, and probably will. Comedy, by way of contrast, remains grounded in reality. Its characters are not meant to be suspect; they are plausible reconstructions of human beings with motives that make sense to a spectator.

From: John Gassner/Edward Quinn (eds.), *The Reader's Encyclopedia of World Drama* (London: Methuen 1970, pp. 262–265).

In an article *A Study of the British in Bed,* Ben Travers, "the grand old man of British farce", gives his view on the difference between comedy and farce:

"So where does the difference between comedy and farce lie? It lies, or should lie, in the story. In the old days farce characters did not represent real people in their behaviour, appearance, dress, speech, or even in their names. By the time I began to write farces I realised they became much more convincing, and funnier, if the characters were recognisable human beings – in short, just the kind of people as in comedy. But whereas in comedy all that happens is quite likely or liable to happen, in farce these same ordinary, everyday people get plunged into preposterous, out-of-this world embarrassments, tribulations and dangers. Trouble must always be the theme, and the deeper the trouble the funnier the farce.

It is in our nature to laugh at imaginary and fictitious tragedy; perhaps it serves to get the tragedies of real life out of our systems. And in farce there must be no half-measures.

... Alan Ayckbourn is well aware of the funny side of misfortune. All his characters have constant worries or difficulties of their own ... But they don't get landed with the desperate, outlandish happenings of farce. Ayckbourn remains to my mind essentially a comedy playwright. His people belong to a cross-section of our populace well-known to us, all-ordinary husbands and wives and their relatives, friends and neighbours, living in reasonably comfortable circumstances in town or the residential suburbs.

What's so funny about them? I think it is the simple fact that Ayckbourn has realised above anyone else that every human being is, in the true sense of the word, unique. There is only one of each of us (in some cases you may think quite enough, too). And we each possess our own personal habits and peculiarities. I have mine, you have yours, so have your parents and relations (especially your Aunt Emmy). So has the vicar, the woman next door, everybody. We may laugh at them to begin with in a kindly sort of way, but we get so accustomed to them that we soon take them for granted. It is this "uniqueness", these everyday habits and mannerisms in each of us, which Ayckbourn rediscovers and delights us with. Watching his plays you keep saying: 'Oh, yes, that's exactly what my sister Jane does, I'd quite forgotten ...'"

From: *TV Times*, 27 September – 3 October 1980, p. 10.

Comedy and farce mostly spring from unusual situations, coincidences, accidents, fleeting moments. There are no real characters in a farce, most of them are overdrawn and have been reduced to one specific character trait. There is hardly any noticeable development, no action. Thus it is understandable that comic writers very often turn to the short play and use this form of drama as a means of presenting the audience with real people in unreal situations.

An Interview with Alan Ayckbourn

GLAAP: *Confusions* is a collection of five plays: *Mother Figure, Drinking Companion, Between Mouthfuls, Gosforth's Fête* and *A Talk in the Park*. In the Author's Note in the Samuel French edition of *Confusions* you point out that the five plays, "although loosely linked, can of course be performed individually".

AYCKBOURN: I'll give a little history of how they were written. In fact, *Mother Figure* was written before the other four. I was asked to write a play for a company to perform. It was going to be a follow-up of a series of plays called *Mixed Doubles* which we did some years ago. A lot of writers got together, including Harold Pinter and James Saunders, and we did a series of one-act plays about marriage, and this new series was supposed to be *Mixed Blessings* and was going to be about children, and parents and children. I wrote *Mother Figure* for this series. The series itself was tried out very briefly in Sussex and didn't work. But I snatched back my play *Mother Figure* and thought one day I might write my own evening, maybe not about children but when I've got some more ideas for one-act plays. So later I sat down and I wrote four plays to accompany *Mother Figure,* using that as the first play to make an evening of *Confusions.* I then had a company of five actors. It was a time in Scarborough when we were trying to extend our winter season and we couldn't stay in Scarborough because there wasn't anywhere for us to play at that point. I wanted to keep the company together. So I arranged for a tour of small theatres around the North of England and I wrote this show. It was fairly flexible and didn't need a lot of setting; we did it very simply. And it was written, as I say, for the five actors in the company. I was a little bit too sure of their abilities to do five one-act plays, and it gave them, I think, a total of 23 parts. And so, in a sense, the whole evening started with *Mother Figure* and as the evening went on they varied and changed their characters and wigs and things, and right at the very end we came to *A Talk in the Park* which was a very slow winding-down of the evening. The play before *A Talk in the Park* was a play called *Gosforth's Fête* which is a very big, quite broad farce and then we suddenly go back to a very quiet, slightly introspective, reflective piece. I think the nice thing about the production was that suddenly one was aware that on the stage, sitting very quietly on four park benches, were the entire cast for the evening, all isolated on their own. It made a very nice finish to the play. So in a sense they are five different plays and they can of course be done individually, in pairs, in threes or whatever, but it was also, of course, intended that, if they are done together, they should be presented in the order in which they appear in the Samuel French edition.

G.: Is there anything that you would like to give a special mention in the introduction to the Students' Book of *Confusions*?

A.: If there was something, it would be a little about how and why they were written. It's important that they are written by – if you like it – a working dramatist who works in a theatre which he happens to direct. They were written originally for a company to perform. They were written, I hope, to show many facets of human behaviour. They are meant to be, of course, entertaining, I hope, other things beside. The thing I just described about how they were devised and written is important. I wouldn't want to make great claims for any of them – let those be made by other people.

G.: Should we stick to the order *Mother Figure, Between Mouthfuls* and *A Talk in the Park*? I'm asking this because when dealing with the three plays in class we did it the other way around. We started with *Mother Figure* and *A Talk in the Park* in order to illustrate the intermediate function and position of *Between Mouthfuls*. But it would probably be more in line with your concept to stick to the original order and have *A Talk in the Park* as the very last.

A.: I like *A Talk in the Park* at the end and I think it has a sort of – as I say – a sort of dying fall on it as a play. It is a little bit like a fugue – once you can see the pattern developing, it has a sort of inevitability about it, and I like that. I think it's a difficult play to follow, certainly on the stage. One's talking about two different things really – about a book and about a stage production. I would say I'm less experienced as far as books go than I am about staging. I would have no hesitation were I going to stage the three plays that I would put *A Talk in the Park* last. I think that to finish with *Between Mouthfuls* would be wrong. I would feel that the evening had started high, then gone down, then gone up again; it would have rather a satisfying curve to it; the graph would be right. In fact those three plays retain the original graph of the evening.

G.: Your plays reflect characteristic features, even eccentricities and whimsicalities, of the people belonging to the so-called middle classes in England. What are the most prominent characteristics of these people?

A.: This is a very difficult and very knotty problem. If you asked a Trotskyite what middle classes were like in England or a Duke you would probably get two very different answers. The middle class is an enormous class, and I think, an increasingly spreading class. I once made a semi-facetious remark that in England half the country were middle-class and the other half were trying to become so. I think the middle classes are best summed up as being the wedge of people between the purely aristocratic class of persons, which one can fairly clearly define – those of good breeding, the Lady Diana Spencers and Prince Charleses of this world – and the other end of the scale. There is the working class, and a very proud, independent body that is. However, I think it is fair to say that there is a constant shuffling of people between the middle and the working classes, mostly of the working going to the middle rather than vice versa. It is undoubtedly true that we are moving inexorably towards a classless society. I suspect that there are many people in the country now who are working-class, who claim to be middle-class when it suits them. In the broadest of terms we would say that the working class is defined as the manual worker. The middle class at the very lowest end – and I do deal with the entire spectrum – are the people who have most recently arrived there.

Plays of mine such as *Absent Friends* or even *Just Between Ourselves* are at the lower end. At the other end of the middle class one has the characters that you see in a play like *The Norman Conquests* who are in fact drifting downwards in the social scale; the money they once had they no longer have.

I was born in the middle of the middle class. It is wrong to say I was born, I was brought up in the middle of the middle class. I was born the son of a musician and a writer, which rather put me outside the class structure, because artists of any type, whether interpretive or creative, have never quite been classed; they are classless and rather suspicious people. Because of a change of parents – I had a step-father who was a bank manager, and a bank manager, of course, is right in the middle of the middle class – and living in Sussex, which is of course a very middle-class area, I suppose, in the whole of my childhood up to the age of fifteen or sixteen, I saw nothing but middle-class people and middle-class situations. It was moving North, where the stronghold of the working class is, that I saw the other side of the coin. Although there is a very strong middle-class area here, the emphasis is much more on manual work. This is the great mining area. The men who live in my immediate vicinity are fishermen.

G.: In terms of *Confusions* would you consider Harry or Terry or Mr Pearce to be middle-class on the basis of what you have just pointed out?

A.: Mr and Mrs Pearce are at one end of the scale; they certainly are the upper end of the middle class. Harry is at the other end. I suppose the restaurant in *Between Mouthfuls* is a middle-class restaurant – the lower end of middle-class restaurants. I once spent an evening in Devonshire and we drove up quite on spec to a hotel. There was a hotel just like this with one waiter and apparently no food that was edible – just this empty restaurant with about five of us in it. That gave me the idea for that. This had obviously once been a wonderful place to eat, but now only people who were passing through the town and didn't know any better – travelling salesmen and people like that – went into the place. The local people, obviously, were eating somewhere else, miles away. We said, ah, this looks like the best hotel, we'll stay here and treat ourselves to a nice meal. That was the background to that. It was a nice hotel but the chef left five years ago and the manager left and all staff had been fired and so there was just this one waiter coping.

G.: That partly answers another of my questions – whether or not the places of action in *Confusions* go back to personal experiences or are products of your imagination.

A.: *Mother Figure* – yes, that's based entirely upon my wife bringing up two children and being at home while I was at work. I observed with some alarm although I think I've exaggerated it in the play, but having spoken to other women I don't think I have exaggerated as much as I thought I had – the fact that if an intelligent woman spends her days exclusively with children she can very easily disappear. It's said in a satirical way, but it is an alarming fact. Having children is one of the easiest things in the world. It often happens by accident and often people say it very glibly. But the implications of a child, if you follow it through, are seventeen years of your life. Often people say, as if it were a dog, "it would be nice to have a baby", meaning, yes, it would be nice to have a baby for six months, and here I suppose is the result of two people saying, "it would be nice to have children". The man thinks, it would be nice to perpetuate his seed, and the woman, that it would be nice to have something to play with. Then, when the whole thing happens, he decides that it isn't exactly what he imagined and disappears to some distant pub to drink with strange women in strange restaurants or strange hotels. And she suddenly finds that she can't get down the drive because the child is going to fall into a fire if she does. Either she takes them all with her or she stays at home. Their lives have been totally changed. Women with children, and I'm not saying that it's a bad thing, talk about children. They are together, and this is the only experience they have. Perhaps it's nice but it's also sad that everything has been narrowed down to that.

In *Drinking Companions*, which you are not going to put in the book, but nevertheless – there were two girls who I observed working in a hotel in Scarborough over the summer. They were there to sell a brand of cigarette and you would see them in the streets, amazingly glamorous, lots of make-up on, hair, nails and eye-lashes all done up. They would approach people in the street and say: "Do you smoke this brand? Would you like to try one?" In the evening they stayed at one of the best hotels in the area. Because my house was having one or two things done to it we – Heather [Ayckbourn's girl-friend] and I – moved into the hotel for about three weeks. We were in our bedroom when I suddenly saw across the courtyard a very ordinary looking woman sitting in the window with a mirror. This was at 5.30. I went away and did a few things and had a sleep and I looked out of the window afterwards and she was still in the window, still making-up, but by now her face had grown and I recognized it as one of these girls. She'd obviously come home, had a bath, taken off her make-up and was now painting for the evening – the evening ritual – the most amazing layers of paint. I got fascinated. Every night I would look out of the window and every night she would do this for about an hour and a half. If I was very quick, I could see her leave the window, I could run out of my room into the lounge, and she would arrive at the top of the stairs, now in her civilian clothes. She'd swing down the stairs with her friend and they'd find some man. The hotel is famous for its salesmen, all looking for a bit of skirt. They would then ply these girls with drinks and probably a meal. I watched these two operate and they were so slick. I can't imagine how they lived because these men would talk and talk and talk and the girls would say, "Yes, I'll have the same drink again, thank you". Between them they would operate. One would look at the other and they would almost nod and they would both suddenly vanish, leaving the man with a bar bill of thirty pounds, a dinner bill, and nothing. Four or five nights a week this would occur. They would play the man off, they would do what they wanted, ... but the price they paid was two and a half hours of his conversation. He would get progressively drunk and he would talk almost word for word like a character.

The third play, *Between Mouthfuls,* which I wrote a long time ago was a television play called *Service Not Included,* the only original television play I ever wrote. It was a half-hour play and it went out on BBC 2 and disappeared. I hate wasting ideas. It was about a waiter. The camera was the waiter and it followed him around a conference, with all sorts of goings-on. It was another hotel – people going off with each other's wives and swindling each other. He apparently heard all this but didn't notice. I've always been fascinated by waiters – how much they hear at a table and how much they don't show. So I translated this very roughly into stage terms. It was the same thing, the camera moving in or the microphone, picking up the conversation and moving away.

Gosforth's Fête [the fourth play]. Here I wanted to write a farce. I wrote a lot of traditional elements into this play. It has all the characters in it that can be found in any traditional English farce – the funny Scout-master, the bluff-leading man, the village spinster, and the authority-figure who usually gets covered in custard pie or, in my case, he gets thrown in the mud – a traditional farce with a lot of ins and outs. It was an interesting play for me to write, in that we had typed the other four plays first. My working method is that I tend to write in longhand and then dictate straight to Heather who types it. In this case I said to Heather that I hadn't written anything at all but that I had the characters. I was going to try, for once – because I knew the structure which was very simple and had a shape – just speaking straight to her. Improvisation. There are five improvisations, corrected afterwards and sometimes rewritten but nevertheless that's how it started. It's fairly clear what it is saying; there is nothing complicated about it as a play. It was intended as an end-piece to the whole evening and is also supposed to say something about what's gone before. So that's really the history.

G.: There seems to be a difference, as far as the structure of the different plays is concerned, particularly between *Mother Figure* and *Between Mouthfuls,* in the sense that in *Mother Figure* you've isolated domestic habits and then enlarged them to the limit of farcical extravagance, on the other hand in *Between Mouthfuls* the play remains on a level that could be considered true to reality more than the others. Is this only our impression?

A.: In order to avoid monotony each play has its own style. It's quite a difficult thing to direct and a very difficult thing to act. The actors have told me that you have to re-adjust in the few seconds between each play. The first play *[Mother Figure]* starts with naturalism and accelerates into a maniac accentuation of the problem, becoming something slightly bizarre. The second play, *Drinking Companions*, is a very naturalistic piece. Staging this production is difficult and is a pure exercise in naturalism. One feels by the end of it that one's been with the man for at least three hours. The third piece *[Between Mouthfuls]* has a style of its own. It is not naturalistic but, of course, it is full of convention. When I staged it, I staged it without real scenery. It was imaginary food. The cutlery and the crockery were real and the wine bottle was real, but mostly for economy, but also because one didn't want to take it into the realms of pure naturalism. It was nice to see the waiter cluttered up with things but it wasn't necessary for him to have food all over the place. We used a simplified version. The convention of voices fading away as he moved away is a convention which is naturalistic, but one which in playing does need an attack which is much sharper than you would need in the preceding play. It is actually a farce and it needs the attack of a farce. What one says about it is – and in playing it I've found in the two versions that I've been involved in – you can go as fast as the waiter can go.

Another influence that drew me to it was Commedia dell'Arte. Years and years ago, when I was about seventeen, I got into a theatre in Edinburgh that I couldn't afford to go to. Somebody sneaked me in in the side-door to see the Piccolo Theatre of Milan do one of their traditional pieces *A Servant of Two Masters*. It was the first time I had seen such physical dexterity on stage – the scene where he serves two masters behind two screens. They throw plates at him which he catches and juggles them on his knees and on his fingers. It was just staggering. Not that I would expect my company to do this. This was a man who had been trained in the tradition. It was something he had grown up with. We couldn't expect to do that in three weeks' rehearsal. But in a sense there is a similarity – a man serving two masters.

Gosforth, as I said, is a pure farce, and the last play *[A Talk in the Park]* brings us down again into naturalism, although having said that, there's a stylisation, a formalisation about it that is not naturalistic. It is purely artificial that one person should move from one bench to the next and although the dialogue itself is naturalistic, perhaps the presentation is less so. And so each play, without jarring with one another, has to find its own level.

G.: *A Talk in the Park* being some sort of epilogue or summary? It epitomizes what has been said before, doesn't it?

A.: In a strange way which I don't know exactly how to describe. One can do two things with a play. One can either surprise people constantly – so they say, I thought it was going to be X but it turned out to be Y, but in this play the best way to describe it is that it is an inevitable play. Once you perceive the circle... I mean, the characters are labelled A, B, C, D, E, although they've all got names. That made it sound very strange and East European. You're into very strange Kafka territory which you don't want to get into. But nevertheless, A does move to B, who then moves to C, who moves to D, who moves to E, and then back to A. So there was a gentle progression which an audience's mind could perceive. The exercise was not so much in what would happen but how it would happen. Could one perceive with the actors the finish? There is a perceivable end to the show which was interesting to me in that one spends much of one's life writing imperceivable endings, saying, well I never quite expected that it would finish like that. There is also satisfaction in resolution, like in music you expect the chord and it happens.

G.: Why did you call the collection *Confusions*? The plays deal with human eccentricities – loneliness, isolation, lack or loss of communication.

A.: It's a word that can mean many things. In English a confused person can be a very unhappy person, can be a very sad person. It can in some cases mean a certain mental disturbance as well. At its other end it can also mean, like in confused identity, very farcical, very silly, very funny. It has a feeling perhaps, as in the title, that it's fun. But I hope, as there are other meanings to the word confusion, there are other levels to the plays which people can find if they want to. It needed a one-word title. As you say, I didn't want *Five Short Plays* or an *Exercise in Five Acts*. There's a great resistance in theatre-goers to one-act plays. One always used to say as a theatre manager or his director that one-act plays were never very popular with audiences, so I wanted to give an illusion at least to the person buying the ticket that this was an evening. I believe that when we first did them it was because this was a team of five actors that in themselves were an entity. I might comment that because of the system in the commercial theatre, as opposed to our theatre, the star actors tend to take the big parts and the small actors take small parts, with the result that the thing becomes overbalanced. What was nice about the original was that the actor for instance who played the waiter in *Drinking Companions*, which was a small part – two lines – the rest of the time he's bringing drinks on and off and he's a background figure, suddenly is drawn forward in the third scene and really becomes a central figure. It was an idea I wanted to pursue more of turning an object, like a three-dimensional sculpture, to the viewer from a different angle. This is something I have noticed that visual artists like to do – they'll say, from this angle the person's nose is the most important feature but if you move around a little the heel or the knee is suddenly important, and the whole picture takes on a totally different aspect. I think it would be interesting to write a play whereby you explore – I did it a little in *The Norman Conquests,* but this was in terms of rooms – in terms of full perspective, perhaps in the way that *Rashomon* was done – saying from this aspect how different the scene looks.

G.: *Mother Figure:* Could you give us your own interpretation of the title? What are, to your mind, the most important associations of the word 'figure' with reference to this play? If you look it up in a dictionary, there are at least five or six connotations. Does 'mother figure' mean that she is a symbol of what mothers in those situations are like or how would you describe it?

A.: Like most of my titles it's an existing phrase whereby a mother figure is literally the image of motherhood. One describes such people as 'mother figures'. It's a phrase I used literally.

G.: I've thought about Terry quite a lot. Could his function in the play be compared with the waiter in *Between Mouthfuls,* on the one hand, or Arthur in *A Talk in the Park* on the other? The impression I came across is that Terry, and the waiter specifically, are some sort of catalyst – interfering, yet not really participating, in what's going on. Would you go along with that?

A.: Funnily enough, the waiter and Terry were played originally by the same actor. I really wanted to show, in the lightest way, that we had in Lucy a sort of extreme woman, exaggerated by her domestic cage. We have here in Terry the most aggressive male with interests in football and who treats women badly. Indeed what I liked most about that is that those sort of men are often most susceptible to the domination of the Lucy mother figure.

I was very amused, only last year, when I went to a cricket match in Scarborough. There were a lot of big fellows in the crowd getting aggressive and starting to throw things. The police were very wary about going in and a little tiny policewoman, about five foot, three inches tall, round, plump, little thing, marched into the middle of them and just snatched the things away and told them to sit down – and they all sat down. She marched away and I thought: "That's wonderful, that's the real clever use of a policewoman". They laughed and sang and she defused them and if they'd sent a man in there, there could have been a very ugly scene. She treated them like naughty children. And that is exactly what this woman does to Terry.

G.: Talking about Lucy, there is Terry's statement: "... you can't put a man in a cage. You try to do that, you've lost him" with Lucy rejoining: "That can apply to women, too, surely?". I think it's about the only time in the whole play that Lucy says this kind of thing.

A.: Yes, I'll tell you. Why she never or very rarely answers what he says is because I treated her like a mother listening to her children who, most of the time, lets them ramble on with silly theories, like whether there are fairies in the garden. In this case this man is airing views that for Lucy are palpably ridiculous. She lets most of them go and she almost throws that in – it's very light. I just wanted to show that she was listening to him, but she was ignoring him. He was behaving in such a childish, silly way that he wasn't even worth replying to. He is apparently dominating the scene, apparently sitting with two lesser beings – two women. In his own home he is used to letting them know this and that. Little Rosie just nods and says: "Yes, quite right". If she does argue, he just goes into a fury. Lucy, on the other hand, ignores him. She doesn't even bother to argue with him. On this occasion she just drops it in, dismisses his whole argument in half a sentence. Rosemary has never thought of that before, that in fact you could even treat women as you treat men. It is a liberationist tract in Lucy, without in any way attempting to arouse Rosemary's consciousness. If there is a fault it's probably women conditioning each other, mothers conditioning daughters in believing their role to be this. In this case Rosemary has obviously been conditioned to believe that everything Terry says – all this rubbish – is correct. One hopes that she has gone away with something new, so perhaps has Terry.

G.: Mr Poddle – what does this name suggest?

A.: It's a doll.

G.: Any doll? Or do you call specific dolls "Mr Poddle"?

A.: No. Obviously by the time Mr Poddle is mentioned Rosemary has become another child because she's sitting up a little later than the other three. You adjust your language to the children's level to a certain extent. There are things you start to call by other names because the children call them that. A lot of parents become practically incomprehensible because, instead of doing the normal thing, which is to teach the children the right words, they say the wrong words and the whole thing becomes more and more convoluted. In the production Mr Poddle is usually a rag-doll of some sort which Lucy uses to cheer Rosemary up. Presumably this is how she cheers her children up. Mr Poddle doesn't like to see people crying. In fact it rings bells in Rosemary's childish subconsciousness. She remembers some other mother years ago, doing just that – in the same way that parents take children's mind off a bad knee or an upset. Sometimes it's a toy, sometimes a teddy bear. Mr Poddle is just an odd doll that she uses with her children.

G.: *Between Mouthfuls* seems to be a broken exercise in collage to me. Could you please explain how the attention of the audience can be directed away from the characters technically because usually the attention of the audience is supposed to be concentrated on the characters?

A.: When the waiter is in proximity of any characters, their level of vocalisation is high enough for one to hear. What one tends to do in production is rather as if they were being faded up on a volume control on a mixer. As the waiter gets closer, they fade up and their performances increase; as he moves away from their table, they never go into a freeze, they just drop down to a level which is no longer interesting. At the same time you bring the waiter's level up to a level where he is interesting all the time. Obviously it's up to him to remain fairly animated. It is an exercise in direction of the eye. Once an audience has accepted your convention, in this case a play where when the waiter isn't there, you can't hear them and therefore we don't want you really to be very interested. Once you've established that convention, an audience, on the whole, unless they happen to be a particulary unpleasant bunch of people, are very happy to go along with this game for as long as it amuses them. Rather like Mr Poddle. They will say: "Yes, we will accept this convention. This is how you're telling the story."

G.: How would you comment on the relation between Mr Pearce and Martin at the very end of the play? How could it be made plausible to the audience that they are on such friendly terms?

A.: They're not. It's another slightly pro-female, anti-male statement that supposes that a man like Martin, when it comes to it, will sell his wife for promotion. Pearce, on the other hand, is prepared to use such a thing; to use his position and thus use his employee's wife, as part of his *droit de seigneur.* The friendship is a purely laughing-with-the-mouth and not the eyes. Something that happens to all of us is the polarisation of men and women in social engagements. I went into a restaurant the other night and the women were sitting on one side and the men were standing on the other having a drink. One says, maybe, because the men want to talk business – but they're not talking business. I can hear what they're talking about and I can hear all that they're talking about and neither are talking about things that are of no interest to the other but both have chosen to separate it, and it's like a sort of ... suspicion. But it's there slightly in the Pearce/Martin thing – so quite a sinister conspiracy. One senses that the men will, when it comes to it, gang up on the women, and the women on the men, although we don't see that side. We see the men's almost tacit I-know-that-you-know-that-you-know-that-I-know: if you want to get on then you must accept it and vice versa, and now let's have a drink together. I don't like you and if the situation changes I shall kill you but at the moment I have to accept you because you are the man who's going to offer me another £3000 a year and a promotion so I'll drink with you. This is observed by the waiter who thinks: "That's not the way I would treat my wife, but I don't want to get up in the world; I'm happy being a waiter".

G.: *A Talk in the Park* is an accumulation, a series of monologues, so the students wondered why the title was *A Talk in the Park*, in the singular.

A.: For each person it's a talk. If you take each individual's point of view, he has had a talk with somebody. Then there's the often-used phrase 'a walk in the park'. All these titles *Between Mouthfuls, A Talk in the Park, Mother Figure* are phrases; most of my titles are existing phrases or bastardizations of existing phrases. *Mother Figure* is a phrase that is used in ordinary conversation. *Between Mouthfuls* is something one can use; one can say: "I was literally between mouthfuls" when somebody interrupts you midway through a meal. *A Talk in the Park* is a bit like "How the Other Half Loves/Lives" – just a shift.

G.: I take it that Arthur is your spokesman in these plays when he says: "Might as well talk to yourself" right at the very end. Am I right?

A.: I don't know. Arthur gets very near being the writer in his thing about people and observing them. I wouldn't claim to be responsible for the rest of what he says about his life.

G.: Arthur is the only one who really refers to himself using the first person singular and thereby opening up some kind of conversation whereas Beryl, for instance, uses a lot of direct speech referring to other people's plights and quarrels.

A.: She is a younger girl. I suppose Arthur is of indeterminate age. We played *her* as a Scot. She's a working-class girl – tough. Charles is a very thin, faded Englishman. They're all representative samples of people you do see alone in parks. Arthur is the sort of rather eccentric man that you tend to avoid with a strange cardboard-box with things in it. Beryl is the girl on her own, wondering whether to jump into the lake. Charles is the sort of down-at-heel businessman. Doreen is a mad old lady with all those bags that you tend to accumulate. Ernest is a kind of counterpart of Beryl. He is a youngish motorcycle kid. He has probably had to sell his motorbike to keep his wife. He is an ex-rocker.

G.: Why does Beryl refer to the Post Office book?

A.: It's quite a revealing thing to have; it suggests that she doesn't have a bank account, which gives her a certain social level. She wouldn't trust banks or have enough money for them. She comes from a level where mum always went to the Post Office to get her child allowance. If you like, it's another social observation that in general terms working-class people don't have bank accounts.

There was a great rumpus some years ago because employers said that to avoid robberies it would be a good idea to pay workers by cheque. In a lot of factories they said: "No, we don't want cheques. That means banks and we don't like banks because we can't get to them because they are not open when we want them and we don't trust them." It was automatic that people of my social level would open a bank account as soon as they had some money. My wife, whose parents are middle-class, but a lower middle class, never had a bank account till she met me. Another argument was that you could draw money out of banks and if you were not careful you could get into debt. The Post Office people won't let you have any money unless it's in the book. So you can see the girl's background very closely. I suppose there are a lot of subtle cross-references, so that an English audience would say: "Ah! They have that, like they have antimacassars on their armchairs." That puts them in that bracket immediately, just like lace curtains at the windows. There are all sorts of references.

APOLLO: Milton Shulman

THERE are five short playlets in **Confusions** at the **Apollo**, and the only thing they have in common is Alan Ayckbourn's ability as a miniaturist of the absurd.

There are no grotesque clowns or flamboyant gestures in Ayckbourn's comedies. He squints his eye quizzically on the commonplace and without malice reveals the lovably ludicrous in all of us.

The special delight of these anecdotes is the ease with which we can recognise the characters in them. Who has not seen the lonely drunk making a pass at a disinterested girl, been served by a punctilious waiter modelling himself on a stately home butler, attended a village fete where disaster lurks in every hydrangea?

This is the stuff of Ayckbourn's middle-class menagerie – and if we cry with laughter as we peer through the bars, we are also aware that others could just as easily be tossing buns at us.

The most successful anecdote concerns two bitterly quarrelling couples in a hotel restaurant being served by one of those waiters who is a master of obsequious obtrusiveness. Just as the wife at one table has revealed that she has been having an affair with her husband's boss, this paragon of servitude is bowing low and suggesting "Green salad, sir, French dressing?"

John Alderton, his hair looking as if it had been shoeshined, shooting his cuffs and carrying himself as if his backbone had been starched, is the hilarious essence of every aspiring head waiter who will never make it to a grand hotel.

A more delirious farcical piece is called Gosforth's Fete in which Ayckbourn reveals once again his conviction that machines are basically malignant.

Reminding us of all the native inanities of the country fete – the dominating organiser, the rampant Wolf Cubs, the unco-operative weather – he compounds the gruesomeness of such an occasion by having a loudspeaker system reveal sexual infidelity amongst the villagers and a tea-urn that refuses to stop disgorging its steaming contents.

Drinking Companion is a sketch of pure observation with John Alderton giving a marvellous impression of a salesman in a provincial town desperately trying to relieve the tedious hours with drink and seduction. Pauline Collins resists him with beautiful rigid politeness.

The item about a mother figure cowing adults with her maternal authority was overcontrived, and the final play about the need for everyone to talk to people who don't listen was a bit of philosophical whimsy that ended the evening on an unnecessarily flat note.

But you can't win them all. Confusions for most of the time is a joyous experience and Alan Strachan's direction neatly integrates the five different pieces.

He ought, though, to switch the order of his final two plays and send the audience rollicking with laughter into Shaftesbury Avenue.

From: *Evening Standard*, London 20 May 1976

Apollo
'Confusions'

By JOHN BARBER

ALTHOUGH some of Alan Ayckbourn's "Confusions" had me helpless with laughter, I found this an unsatisfying evening. The author's observation is sharp, but he declines to penetrate beneath the surface.

This expert and prolific writer provides five one-act comedies, a form I much enjoy. Two of them come off well, and in both Pauline Collins is both funny and touching.

In the witty "Mother Figure," she plays a wife so brain-washed by small children that she can only baby-talk to visiting adults. In giving two neighbours nursery orders she unknowingly composes a serious difference between them.

Successful, too, in a more familiar vein, is "Gosforth's Fête, " about a disastrous village bun-fight: a storm breaks, the wolf cubs go beserk, and the public-address system relays the tea-lady's confession of her unfortunate pregnancy.

"Between Mouthfuls" is a technically dazzling exercise in collage. We cut back and forth between two warring couples, at different restaurant tables, while an intrusive waiter hovers. Here as elsewhere, Miss Collins shares honours with John Alderton, James Cossins, Sheila Gish and Derek Fowlds.

But the hotel encounter between the drunk and two wary girl is over stretched and unpleasant, as is the final item, a collection of monologues for park-bench bores.

Not even Noel Coward had a sharper ear than Mr Ayckbourn for the tell-tale fib, the unforgivable aside, the unthinking insult that blisters the heart.

But seven foundering marriages in five plays is too much, especially as we never learn what went wrong with one.

The facts are right, and they are funny; but we only care for facts when they explain truths.

Director, Alan Strachan.

From: *Daily Telegraph,* London 20 May 1976

Mother Figure

Lucy's sitting-room

It is a suburban room, fairly untidy, with evidence of small children. There are two doors – one to the kitchen and back door, one to the bedrooms and front door

Lucy hurries in from the bedrooms on her way to the kitchen. She is untidy, unmade-up, in dressing-gown and slippers

The telephone rings

---

suburban room [səˈbɜːbən] room in a house just outside a town
unmade-up *(colloquial)* not wearing make-up (lipstick, powder, etc.)

LUCY *(calling behind her)* Nicholas! Stay in your own bed and leave Sarah alone.

Lucy goes out to the kitchen, returning at once with a glass of water

All right, Jamie, darling. Mummy's coming with a dinkie … *(As she passes the telephone, she lifts the receiver off the rest and almost immediately replaces it)* Mummy's coming, Jamie, Mummy's coming.

Lucy goes off to the bedroom with the glass

The front door chimes sound. A pause, then they sound again

Lucy returns from the bedrooms

Sarah! You're a naughty, naughty girl. I told you not to play with Jamie's syrup. That's for Jamie's toothipegs …

The door chimes sound again

Lucy ignores these and goes off to the kitchen. She returns almost at once with a toilet roll, hauling off handfuls of it as she goes to perform some giant mopping-up operation

Nicholas, if you're not in bed by the time I come up, I shall smack your botty.

There are two rings on the back door bell

Lucy goes off to the bedroom

A pause

---

dinkie *(baby talk)* drink
chimes sound of bells ringing in harmony
toothipegs ['tu:θɪpegz] *(baby talk)* teeth
to haul to pull hard
mopping-up operation using a mop, cloth, paper, etc. to dry s.th. which is wet
to smack to hit with the open hand
botty *(baby talk)* bottom (Popo)

Rosemary, a rather frail, mousey-looking woman, comes in from the kitchen

ROSEMARY *(calling timidly)* Woo-hoo!

Lucy returns from the bedroom

LUCY *(calling as before)* Now go to sleep. At once. *(Seeing Rosemary)* Oh.

ROSEMARY Hallo, I thought you must be in.

LUCY *(puzzled)* Hallo?

ROSEMARY I thought you were in.

LUCY Yes.

ROSEMARY You are.

LUCY Yes.

ROSEMARY Hallo.

LUCY Hallo. *(A slight pause)* Who are you?

ROSEMARY Next door.

LUCY What?

ROSEMARY From next door. Mrs Oates. Rosemary. Do you remember?

LUCY *(vaguely)* Oh, yes. Hallo.

ROSEMARY Hallo. I did ring both bells but nobody seemed …

LUCY No. I don't take much notice of bells.

ROSEMARY Oh.

LUCY I've rather got my hands full.

ROSEMARY Oh yes. With the children, you mean? How are they?

LUCY Fine.

ROSEMARY All well?

LUCY Yes.

ROSEMARY Good. It's three you've got, isn't it?

LUCY Yes.

ROSEMARY Still, I expect it's time well spent.

LUCY I haven't much option.

ROSEMARY No.

LUCY Well.

---

frail not strong
mousey-looking timid and shy-looking
I've got my hands full I'm very busy
I haven't much option I've no alternative

ROSEMARY Oh, don't let me – if you want to get on ...

LUCY No.

ROSEMARY I mean, if you were going to bed.

LUCY Bed?

ROSEMARY *(indicating Lucy's attire)* Well ...

LUCY Oh, no. I didn't get dressed today, that's all.

ROSEMARY Oh. Not ill?

LUCY No.

ROSEMARY Oh.

LUCY I just wasn't going anywhere.

ROSEMARY Oh, well ...

LUCY I haven't been anywhere for weeks.

ROSEMARY That's a shame.

LUCY I don't think I've got dressed for weeks, either.

ROSEMARY Ah. No, well, I must say we haven't seen you. Not that we've been looking but we haven't seen you.

LUCY No. Do you want to sit down?

ROSEMARY Oh, thank you. Just for a minute.

LUCY If you can find somewhere. *(She moves the odd toy)*

ROSEMARY *(sitting)* Yes, we were wondering actually, er, if you were alright, actually. My husband and I – Terry, that's my husband – he was remarking that we hadn't seen you for a bit.

LUCY No.

ROSEMARY We heard the children, of course. Not to complain of, mind you, but we heard them but we didn't see you.

LUCY No. *(She picks up various toys during the following and puts them in the play-pen)*

ROSEMARY Or your husband.

LUCY No.

ROSEMARY But then I said to Terry, if they need us they've only to ask. They know where we are. If they want to keep themselves to themselves, that's all right by us. I mean, that's why they put up that great big fence so they could keep themselves to themselves. And that's all right by us.

---

attire [ə'taɪə] clothes
the odd toy children's playthings lying here and there
for a bit for some time
play-pen Laufstall
to keep oneself to oneself *(colloq.)* to have little to do with other people

LUCY Good.

ROSEMARY And then ten minutes ago, we got this phone call.

LUCY Phone call?

ROSEMARY Yes. Terry answered it – that's my husband – and they say will you accept a transfer charge call from a public phone box in Middlesbrough and Terry says, hallo, that's funny, he says, who do we know in Middlesbrough and I said, not a soul and he says, well, that's funny, Terry says, well who is it? How do we know we know him? And if we don't know him, we don't want to waste money talking to him but if we do, it might be an emergency and we won't sleep a wink. And the operator says, well suit yourself, take it or leave it, it's all the same to me. So we took it and it was your husband.

LUCY Harry?

ROSEMARY Harry, yes. Mr Compton.

LUCY What did he want?

ROSEMARY Well – you. He was worried. He's been ringing you for days. He's had the line checked but there's been no reply.

LUCY Oh.

ROSEMARY Has it not been ringing?

LUCY Possibly. I don't take much notice of bells. *(She goes to listen for the children)*

ROSEMARY Oh. Anyway, he sounded very worried. So I said I'd pop round and make sure. I took his number in case you wanted to …

Lucy is clearly not listening

Are you all right?

LUCY Yes, I was listening for Nicholas.

ROSEMARY Oh. That's the baby?

LUCY No.

ROSEMARY *(warmly)* Ah.

LUCY I'm sorry. I'm being very rude. It's just I haven't – spoken to anyone for days. My husband isn't home much.

ROSEMARY Oh, I quite understand. Would you like his number?

---

transfer charge call telephone call paid for by the person who receives it
emergency suddenly dangerous situation
we won't sleep a wink we shan't be able to sleep at all
to have the line checked to ask the telephone engineer to see if the line is in order
to pop round *(colloq.)* to make a short visit

LUCY What?

ROSEMARY Your husband's telephone number in Middlesbrough. Would you like it? He said he'd hang on. It's from a hotel.

LUCY No.

ROSEMARY Oh.

LUCY Whatever he has to say to me, he can say to my face or not at all.

ROSEMARY Ah. *(Laying a slip of paper gingerly on the coffee-table)* Well, it's there.

LUCY Would you care for a drink or something?

ROSEMARY A drink? Oh – well – what's the time? Well – I don't know if I should. Half past – oh yes, well – why not? Yes, please. Why not? A little one.

LUCY Orange or lemon?

ROSEMARY I beg your pardon?

LUCY Orange juice or lemon juice? Or you can have milk.

ROSEMARY Oh, I see. I thought you meant …

LUCY Come on. Orange or lemon? I'm waiting.

ROSEMARY Is there a possibility of some coffee?

LUCY No.

ROSEMARY Oh.

LUCY It'll keep you awake. I'll get you an orange, it's better for you.

ROSEMARY Oh …

LUCY *(as she goes)* Sit still. Don't run around. I won't be a minute.

Lucy goes out into the kitchen

Rosemary sits nervously. She rises after a second, looks guiltily towards the kitchen and sits again. The door chimes sound. Rosemary looks toward the kitchen. There is no sign of Lucy. The door chimes sound again. Rosemary gets up hesitantly

ROSEMARY *(calling)* Mrs –er …

LUCY *(off, in the kitchen)* Wait, wait, wait! I'm coming …

The door chimes sound again

ROSEMARY Oh. Well, I'd better …

Rosemary runs off to the front door. Lucy returns from the kitchen with a glass of orange juice

---

to hang on *(colloq.)* to wait
gingerly ['dʒɪndʒəlɪ] in a careful, hesitating way

LUCY Here we are, Rosemary, I ... *(She looks round the empty room, annoyed. Calling)* Rosemary! It's on the table.

Lucy puts the orange juice on the coffee-table and goes out to the kitchen again. Rosemary returns from the hall with Terry, a rather pudgy man in shirt sleeves

ROSEMARY *(sotto voce)* Come in a minute.

TERRY I'm watching the telly.

ROSEMARY Just for a minute.

TERRY I wondered where you'd got to. I mean, all you had to do was give her the number ...

ROSEMARY I want you to meet her. See what you think. I don't think she's well.

TERRY How do you mean?

ROSEMARY She just seems ...

TERRY Is she ill?

ROSEMARY I don't know ...

TELLY Well, either she's ill or she isn't.

ROSEMARY Ssh.

Lucy returns from the kitchen with a plate of biscuits

LUCY Here we are now. *(Seeing Terry)* Oh.

TERRY Evening.

LUCY Hallo.

ROSEMARY My husband.

LUCY Terry, isn't it?

TERRY Yes.

LUCY That's a nice name, isn't it? *(Pointing to the sofa)* Sit down there then. Have you got your orange juice, Rosemary?

Terry sits

ROSEMARY Yes, thank you. *(She picks up the glass of orange juice and sits)*

---

annoyed irritated
hall entrance passage of a house
pudgy rather fat
sotto voce ['sɒtəʊ'vəʊtʃɪ] *(Italian)* in a low voice
telly television

TERRY Orange juice?

ROSEMARY Yes.

TERRY What are you doing drinking that?

ROSEMARY I like orange juice.

LUCY Now, here's some very special choccy bics but you mustn't eat them all. I'm going to trust you. *(She starts tidying up again)*

ROSEMARY *(still humouring her)* Lovely. *(She mouths "say something" to Terry)*

TERRY Yes. Well, how are you keeping then – er, sorry, I'm forgetting. Lesley, isn't it?

LUCY Mrs Compton.

TERRY Yes. Mrs Compton. How are you?

LUCY I'm very well, thank you, Terry. Nice of you to ask.

TERRY And what about Har – Mr Compton?

LUCY Very well. When I last saw him. Rosemary dear, try not to make all that noise when you drink.

ROSEMARY Sorry.

TERRY Yes, yes, we were saying that your husband's job obviously takes him round and about a lot.

LUCY Yes. *(She starts folding nappies)*

TERRY Doesn't get home as much as he'd like, I expect.

LUCY I've no idea.

TERRY But then it takes all sorts. Take me, I'm home on the nose six o'clock every night. That's what she wants. Who am I to ...? *(Pause)* Yes, I think I quite envy your husband, sometimes. Getting about a bit. I mean, when you think about it, it's more natural. For a man. His natural way of life. Right back to the primitive. Woman stays in the cave, man the hunter goes off roving at will. Mind you, I think the idea originally was he went off hunting for food. Different sort of game these days, eh?

ROSEMARY *(hissing)* Terry!

---

choccy bics ['tʃɒkɪ 'bɪks] *(baby talk)* chocolate biscuits
to humour someone to take care not to make s.o. excited or angry
his job takes him round and about a lot *(colloq.)* he has to go on a lot of business journeys
nappy *(colloq.)* napkin (Windel)
on the nose six o'clock *(colloq.)* exactly at six o'clock
to get about to travel
roving at will going wherever one likes
to hiss to speak sharply through one's teeth

TERRY Be after something quite different these days, eh? *(He nods and winks)*

LUCY Now don't get silly, Terry.

TERRY What? Ah – beg your pardon.

A pause. Terry munches a biscuit. Rosemary sips her orange juice

ROSEMARY Very pleasant orange juice.

LUCY Full of vitamin C.

TERRY No, I didn't want to give you the wrong impression there. But, but seriously, I was saying to Rosie here, you can't put a man in a cage. You try to do that, you've lost him. See my point?

LUCY That can apply to women, too, surely?

ROSEMARY Yes, quite right.

TERRY What do you mean, quite right?

ROSEMARY Well ...

TERRY You're happy enough at home, aren't you?

ROSEMARY Yes, but – yes – but ...

TERRY Well then, that's what I'm saying. You're the woman, you're happy enough at home looking after that. I'm the man, I have to be out and about.

ROSEMARY I don't know about that. You'd never go out at all unless I pushed you.

TERRY What do you mean? I'm out all day.

ROSEMARY Only because you have to be. You wouldn't be if you didn't have to be. When you don't, you come in, sit down, watch the television and go to bed.

TERRY I have to relax.

ROSEMARY You're always relaxing.

TERRY Now don't deny me relaxing.

ROSEMARY I don't.

TERRY Yes, you do, you just said ...

LUCY Now, don't quarrel. I won't have any quarrelling.

TERRY Eh?

ROSEMARY Sorry.

LUCY Would you like an orange drink as well, Terry? Is that what it is?

---

to munch to break with the teeth and eat
to sip to drink slowly
to push s.o. *here:* to persuade s.o. (to do s.th.)

TERRY Er ... Oh no – I don't go in for that sort of a drink much, if you know what I mean. *(He winks, then reaches for a biscuit)* No, I'll have another one of these biscuits, if you don't mind?

LUCY Just a minute, how many have you had?

TERRY This is my second. It's only my second.

LUCY Well, that's all. No more after that. I'll get you some milk. You better have something that's good for you.

TERRY *(half rising)* Oh no – thank you, not milk, no.

LUCY *(going to the kitchen)* Wait there. *(Seeing Terry has half risen)* And don't jump about while you're eating, Terry.

Lucy goes out to the kitchen

TERRY You're right. She's odd.

ROSEMARY I said she was.

TERRY No wonder he's gone off.

ROSEMARY Perhaps that's why she's odd.

TERRY Why?

ROSEMARY Because he's gone off.

TERRY Rubbish. And we'll have less of that, too, if you don't mind.

ROSEMARY What?

TERRY All this business about me never going out of the house.

ROSEMARY It's true.

TERRY It's not true and it makes me out to be some bloody idle loafer.

ROSEMARY All I said ...

TERRY And even if it is true, you have no business saying it in front of other people.

ROSEMARY Oh, honestly, Terry, you're so touchy. I can't say a thing right these days, can I?

TERRY Very little. Now you come to mention it.

ROSEMARY Niggle, niggle, niggle. You keep on at me the whole time. I'm frightened to open my mouth these days. I don't know what's got

---

I don't go in for ... I don't like ...
odd not normal
rubbish nonsense
idle [aɪdl] **loafer** very lazy person
touchy irritable
to niggle (at s.o.) to criticise s.o.
to keep on at s.o. *(colloq.)* to criticise s.o. continuously

into you lately. You're in a filthy mood from the moment you get up till you go to bed ...

TERRY What are you talking about?

ROSEMARY Grumbling and moaning ...

TERRY Oh, shut up.

ROSEMARY You're a misery to live with these days, you really are.

TERRY I said, shut up.

ROSEMARY *(more quietly)* I wish to God you'd go off somewhere sometimes, I really do.

TERRY Don't tempt me. I bloody feel like it occasionally, I can tell you.

ROSEMARY *(tearfully)* Oh, lovely ...

TERRY If you think I enjoy spending night after night sitting looking at you ... *(He throws the biscuit down)* What the hell am I eating these damn biscuits for ... you're mistaken. Here, give me that – *(Thirsty from the biscuits, he grabs her orange juice glass and drains it in one)*

ROSEMARY That's my orange juice, do you mind. *(She rises and stamps her foot)*

TERRY Come on. Let's go. *(He jumps up)*

ROSEMARY That was my orange juice when you've quite finished.

Lucy enters with a glass of milk

LUCY Now what are you two doing jumping about?

Rosemary sits

TERRY We've got to be going, I'm sorry.

LUCY Not till you've finished. Sit down.

TERRY Listen, I'm sorry we ...

LUCY *(seeing Rosemary's distraught state)* What's the matter with Rosemary?

ROSEMARY *(sniffing)* Nothing ...

TERRY Nothing.

LUCY What have you been doing to her?

---

filthy mood very bad temper
to grumble meckern
misery ['mɪzərɪ] *here:* s.o. who is always unhappy and grumbling
I bloody feel like it *(vulgar)* I really want to do it
to drain (a drink) to finish (a drink)
when you have quite finished *(colloq.)* wenn du gefälligst aufhören würdest
distraught [dɪ'strɔ:t] unhappy and upset

TERRY Nothing.

LUCY Here's your milk.

TERRY Thank you.

LUCY You don't deserve it.

TERRY I don't want it.

LUCY Don't be tiresome.

TERRY I hate the damned stuff.

LUCY I'm not going to waste my breath arguing with you, Terry. It's entirely up to you if you don't want to be big and strong.

TERRY Now, look ...

LUCY If you want to be a little weakling, that's up to you. Just don't come whining to me when all your nails and teeth fall out. Now then, Rosemary, let's see to you. *(She puts down the milk and picks up the biscuits)* Would you like a choccy biccy?

ROSEMARY No, thank you.

LUCY Come on, they're lovely choccy, look. Milk choccy ...

ROSEMARY No, honestly.

TERRY Rosie, are you coming or not?

LUCY Well, have a drink, then. Blow your nose and have a drink, that's a good girl. *(Seeing the glass)* Oh, it's all gone. You've drunk that quickly, haven't you?

ROSEMARY I didn't drink it. He did.

LUCY What?

ROSEMARY He drank it.

LUCY Terry, did you drink her orange juice?

TERRY Look, there's a programme I want to watch ...

LUCY Did you drink Rosemary's orange juice?

TERRY Look, good night ...

ROSEMARY Yes, he did.

LUCY Well, I think that's really mean.

ROSEMARY He just takes anything he wants.

LUCY Really mean.

ROSEMARY Never thinks of asking.

TERRY I'm going.

---

tiresome annoying, irritating
to whine wimmern
to blow one's nose die Nase putzen
mean gemein

LUCY Not before you've apologized to Rosemary.

TERRY Good night.

Terry goes out

LUCY *(calling after him)* And don't you dare come back until you're ready to apologize. *(To Rosemary)* Never mind him. Let him go. He'll be back.

ROSEMARY That's the way to talk to him.

LUCY What?

ROSEMARY That's the way he ought to be talked to more often.

LUCY I'm sorry. I won't have that sort of behaviour. Not from anyone.

ROSEMARY He'll sulk now. For days.

LUCY Well, let him. It doesn't worry us, does it?

ROSEMARY No. It's just sometimes – things get on top of you – and then he comes back at night – and he starts on at me and I … *(She cries)* Oh dear – I'm so sorry – I didn't mean to …

LUCY *(cooing)* Come on now. Come on …

ROSEMARY I've never done this. I'm sorry …

LUCY That's all right. There, there.

ROSEMARY I'm sorry. *(She continues to weep)*

LUCY Look who's watching you.

ROSEMARY Who?

LUCY *(picking up a doll)* Look. Mr Poddle. Mr Poddle's watching you. *(She holds up the doll)* You don't want Mr Poddle to see you crying, do you? Do you?

ROSEMARY *(lamely)* No …

LUCY Do we, Mr Poddle? *(She shakes Mr Poddle's head)* No, he says, no. Stop crying, Rosie. *(She nods Mr Poddle's head)* Stop crying, Rosie. Yes – yes.

Rosemary gives an embarrassed giggle

That's better. Was that a little laugh, Mr Poddle? Was that a little laugh?

Lucy wiggles Mr Poddle about, bringing him close up to Rosemary's face and taking him away again

---

to apologize [əˈpɒlədʒaɪz] to say that one is sorry
I won't have that sort of behaviour I won't allow anyone to behave in that way
to sulk [sʌlk] to say very little because one is in a bad temper
to coo [kuː] to say softly
Mr Poddle child's name for a doll

Was that a little laugh? Was that a little laugh? Was that a little laugh?

Rosemary giggles uncontrollably

Terry enters from the hall and stands amazed

TERRY Er …

Lucy and Rosemary become aware of him

Er – I've locked myself out.

LUCY Have you come back to apologize?

TERRY You got the key, Rosie?

ROSEMARY Yes.

TERRY Let's have it then.

LUCY Not until you apologize.

TERRY Look, I'm not apologizing to anyone. I just want the key. To get back into my own house, if you don't mind. Now, come on.

ROSEMARY *(producing the key from her bag)* Here.

LUCY Rosemary, don't you dare give it to him.

TERRY Eh?

ROSEMARY What?

LUCY Not until he apologizes.

TERRY Rosie, give me the key.

LUCY No, Rosemary. I'll take it. Give it to me.

TERRY Rosie.

LUCY Rosemary.

ROSEMARY *(torn)* Er …

LUCY *(very fiercely)* Rosemary, will you give me that key at once.

Rosemary gives Lucy the key. Terry regards Lucy

Thank you.

TERRY Would you mind most awfully giving me the key to my own front door?

LUCY Certainly.

---

torn *here:* not able to decide
fierce [fɪəs] angry
would you mind most awfully …? *(very polite and ironic)* would you have anything against …?

TERRY Thank you so much.

LUCY Just as soon as you've apologized to Rosemary.

TERRY I've said, I'm not apologizing to anyone.

LUCY Then you're not having the key.

TERRY Now listen, I've got a day's work to do tomorrow. I'm damned if I'm going to start playing games with some frustrated nutter …

ROSEMARY Terry …

LUCY Take no notice of him, Rosemary, he's just showing off.

TERRY Are you going to give me that key or not?

LUCY Not until you apologize.

TERRY All right. I'll have to come and take it off you, won't I?

LUCY You try. You just dare try, my boy.

TERRY All right. *(He moves towards Lucy)*

ROSEMARY Terry …

LUCY Just you try and see what happens.

TERRY *(halted by her tone; uncertainly)* I'm not joking.

LUCY Neither am I.

TERRY Look, I don't want to … Look, just give me the key, there's a good …

LUCY Not until you apologize to Rosemary.

TERRY Oh, for the love of … All right *(To Rosemary)* Sorry.

LUCY Say it nicely.

TERRY I'm very sorry, Rosie. Now give us the key, for God's sake.

LUCY When you've drunk your milk. Sit down and drink your milk.

TERRY Oh, blimey … *(He sits)*

LUCY That's better.

TERRY I hate milk.

LUCY Drink it up.

Terry scowls and picks up the glass.

ROSEMARY *(putting her tongue out, unseen by Lucy)* Yeeeurr –

Terry bangs down his glass and moves as if to hit her

---

nutter *(slang)* crazy person
to show off to make oneself seem more important than one really is
blimey ['blaɪmɪ] *(vulgar)* exclamation of surprise, irritation, etc. (from 'God blind me')
to scowl [skaʊl] to frown, showing bad temper

TERRY Don't you –!
ROSEMARY Ah!
LUCY Terry!
TERRY She stuck her tongue out at me.
LUCY Sit still.
TERRY But she …
LUCY Sit!

Terry sits scowling. Rosemary smirks at him smugly

(Seeing her) And don't do that, Rosemary. If the wind changes, you'll get stuck like it. And sit up straight and don't slouch.

Rosemary does so

TERRY *(taking a sip of the milk)* This is horrible.

Silence. He takes another sip

It's warm.

Silence. Another sip

TERRY There's a football international on television, you know.
LUCY Not until you've drunk that up, there isn't. Come on, Rosemary. Help Terry to drink it. "Georgie Porgie Pudding and Pie, Kissed the girls and …?"
ROSEMARY "Made them cry."
LUCY Good.
ROSEMARY / LUCY "When the boys came out to play, Georgie Porgie ran away." *(Speaking together)*
TERRY *(finishing his glass with a giant swallow)* All gone. *(He wipes his mouth)*
LUCY Good boy.
TERRY Can I have the key now, please?

---

to stick one's tongue out to show that one has a low opinion of s.o. by putting out one's tongue
to smirk to smile slightly
smugly in a self-satisfied way
to slouch [slaʊtʃ] opposite of 'to sit up straight'
Georgie Porgie Pudding and Pie, Kissed the girls and made them cry Children's nonsense rhyme. Spoken here to encourage Terry to drink the milk.
with a giant swallow without stopping until the glass is empty

LUCY Here you are.

Terry goes to take it

What do you say?

TERRY Thank you.

LUCY All right. Off you go, both of you.

ROSEMARY *(kissing her on the cheek)* Night night.

LUCY Night night, dear. Night, night, Terry.

TERRY *(kissing Lucy likewise)* Night night.

LUCY Sleep tight.

TERRY Hope the bugs don't bite.

LUCY Hold Rosemary's hand, Terry.

Rosemary and Terry hold hands

See her home safely.

TERRY Night.

ROSEMARY Night.

LUCY Night night.

Terry and Rosemary go off hand in hand

(With a sigh) Blooming kids. Honestly.

The telephone rings. Lucy, as she passes it, picks it up and replaces it as before

Honestly ...

---

bug Wanze. 'Sleep tight. Hope the bugs don't bite' is a rhyme sometimes spoken to small children at bed-time.

blooming exclamation to express irritation, anger, etc., similar to 'bloody' but less strong (‚verflixt')

Introducing the Play

Lucy and Harry Compton, a married couple with three small children, live in the suburbs. Owing to his job Mr Compton spends a lot of time away from home whereas Lucy rarely leaves the house due to her full-time occupation of bringing up the children. Both her sole occupation with the children and her husband's continual absence from home have resulted in Lucy isolating herself from the outside world. As a result she has lost interest both in her appearance and dress, and by severing herself from her environment and neighbours has forgotten the language and behaviour patterns of adults; she doesn't even answer the telephone or door any more. When her neighbours, Rosemary and Terry, call one day to tell her that her husband has been trying to phone her and was rather concerned, Lucy only replies in monosyllables. Whereas Lucy addresses them by their Christian names, she wishes herself and her husband to be called Mr and Mrs Compton. A further indication that she is treating them like children is underlined by the fact that she offers them orange juice and milk and scolds them as naughty children when a difference of opinion arises between them. It transpires that Rosemary is not very happy with her own domestic situation as her husband, Terry, does not seem to lead a very social life and spends most of his leisure time in front of the television. Although in the beginning Lucy appears a little odd to Rosemary, both women understand each other because of their mutual isolation from their respective husbands and environment. In the course of a short time Rosemary even succumbs to Lucy's motherliness and reacts in a child-like way. Unlike his wife, Terry blankly refuses to be dominated by Lucy and only goes along with her as far as is necessary to obtain his house-key from Rosemary. Yet in the very end, he too succumbs to Lucy.

Analysing the Text

THEMES – STATEMENTS – QUESTIONS – QUOTATIONS

Suggestions and guidelines which can be used as starting points for classroom work and discussion. First numbers ("▷") refer to the pages in the Students' Book, numbers in brackets refer to the lines.

Aspects of isolation

– in the suburbs "Who are you? Next door. What?"	▷ 10 (14–16)
– from the neighbours "That's why they put up that great big fence."	▷ 11 (32)
– in marriage "My husband isn't home much."	▷ 12 (31)

Discussion prompt:
Is the playwright making a serious point in the play or just amusing the audience?

Husband and wife relationships

– "Take me, I'm home on the nose six o'clock every night."	▷ 15 (23)
– "You can't put a man in a cage."	▷ 16 (9)
– "That can apply to women, too, surely?"	▷ 16 (11)
– "Niggle, niggle, niggle."	▷ 17 (29)
– See also	▷ 16 (20–30), 18 (6), 18 (16), 20 (7), 23 (4)

Discussion prompt:
Would it be truer to say that Ayckbourn is showing us how childish adult problems are, or how childish adults can be?

Motherhood and Fatherhood

– "I haven't much option."	▷ 10 (30)
– "I haven't been anywhere for weeks."	▷ 11 (12)
– "I'm sorry. I'm being very rude. It's just I haven't – spoken to anyone for days. My husband isn't home much."	▷ 12 (30)
– "Man the hunter goes off roving at will."	▷ 15 (28)

Discussion prompt:
The most distressing element of Lucy's dilemma is her isolation from

all adult contact. The male characters reserve for themselves the right to opt out of family restraints. Lucy's husband is rarely at home. Terry, although physically present, maintains the rights of "man the hunter".

Ayckbourn makes this point by means of the conventions of farce. Could he have presented this idea with equal or greater effect if he had chosen a different dramatic form?

Lucy's language

– only talks to the children	
– her baby talk does not qualify her for the adult world any more	
– "Come on, they're lovely choccy, look. Milk choccy."	▷ 19 (16)
– "Look who's watching you ... Look. Mr Poddle."	▷ 20 (20–22)
– See also	▷ 17 (10), 18 (24), 19 (8), 19 (25), 20 (10), 23 (9), 23 (10), 23 (17)

Discussion prompt:
Lucy speaks to her neighbours as if they were naughty children. Find examples of this in the text and try to categorize them. For example expressions of encouragement, command, cajolement, etc.

Lucy's appearance and behaviour

– "Oh, no. I didn't get dressed today, that's all."	▷ 11 (6)
– "I don't take much notice of bells."	▷ 12 (20)
– "Orange juice or lemon juice? Or you can have milk."	▷ 13 (15)
– "Come on, Rosemary. Help Terry to drink it."	▷ 23 (17)

Discussion prompt:
Lucy clearly does not realize the absurdity of her behaviour. How do you account for this a) in realistic terms? b) in terms of farce?

Levels of communication

- Lucy's communication with
  a) her children, b) Terry, c) Rosemary
- "Nicholas, if you're not in bed by the time I come up, I shall smack your botty." ▷ 9 (17)
- "And don't jump about while you're eating, Terry." ▷ 17 (10)
- "Now then, Rosemary, let's see to you ... would you like a choccy biccy?" ▷ 19 (12)

Discussion prompt:
Compare the reaction of Rosemary and Terry to Lucy's unusual treatment. What does this tell us about their characters and how they communicate with, and relate to, other people?

From realism into farce

a) "I don't take much notice of bells." ▷ 12 (20)

As illustrated in the outline (p. 42), Lucy lets nothing distract her from her role as a mother figure, neither the telephone, the door bell, nor the neighbours. Ironically, it is just these interruptions which mark the stages in the play. After each sound effect, the action moves a step further into the realm of farce, finishing in pure farce after Mr Poddle's squeak. Just before each sound effect, the dialogue gives the audience a hint of the following development.

Discussion prompt:
What role do bells, chimes and squeaks from children's toys (cf. Cassette) play in the development of the action from realism into farce?

b) "That was my orange juice when you've quite finished." ▷ 18 (19)

From this point on Rosemary and Terry behave more and more like children, and Rosemary develops a little spirit of rebellion, prompted by Lucy's example in dealing with Terry. Rosemary's outburst, however, takes a childish turn: she sticks her tongue out.

Discussion prompt:
Can the above quotation be considered a turning point in the action?

Blackboard:

		Action		View of Motherhood
First step: Telephone rings Door chimes (Students' Book, pages 8–9)	→	Realistic setting	→	Realistic – harrassed housewife and mother
↓				
Second step: Two rings at the back door (Students' Book, page 9)	→	Matter-of-fact – slowly developing a slight tendency towards farce	→	Matter-of-fact – developing slowly into exaggeration with elements of farce
↓				
Third step: Door chimes (Students' Book, page 13)	→	Increasingly farcical	→	Increasing distortion in the direction of farce
↓				
Fourth step: Mr Poddle's squeak (see Cassette, cf. Students' Book, page 20)	→	Pure farce	→	Pure farce

Presenting the Cassette

Are sound effects essential or only embellishments?

The opening moments of *Mother Figure* are dominated by sound effects. Students could first discuss whether these can be left out, or if this would be detrimental to the scene. The discussion need not, at this stage, come to any firm conclusion. The following experiment can then be tried. Groups of students could prepare a reading or recording, without sound effects, of pages 8–10 in the Students' Book, as far down as line 30. They can then compare their version with the Cassette, and discuss the difference.

The Cassette makes it clear that we are being presented with a very naturalistic scene, that the telephone and door bells are unwelcome interruptions to an already harrassed housewife and mother who is run off her feet. It is essential that the realistic setting should be established at the very beginning of the play, to lull the audience into a false sense of security and make them at first accept the following somewhat bizarre events as plausible.

Is a script open to different interpretations?

Mother Figure is made up of little cameo scenes, e.g. Rosemary's recital about the telephone call (Students' Book, pp. 11–12); Rosemary's decision to have a drink (Students' Book, p. 13); and so on through the whole play.

These scenes lend themselves readily to student productions, the class dividing into groups and deciding how they would tackle the production, especially where they would place the stress and how they would deal with the intonation and pacing. These versions can then be compared with each other. A comparison with the Cassette could lead to further useful discussion and make students listen more attentively for differences and nuances.

Furniture and Property List

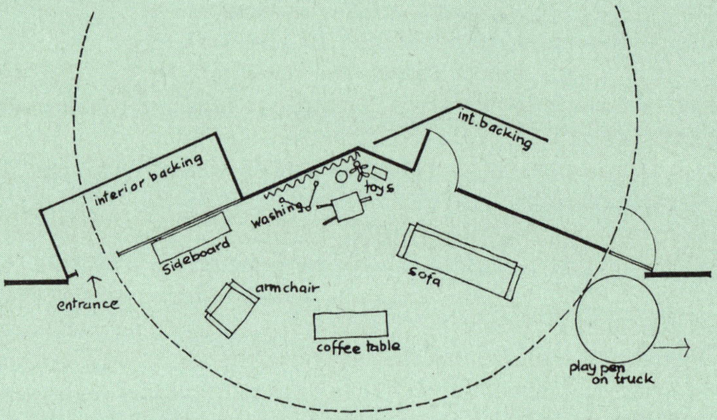

Mother Figure

On stage: Sofa. *On it:* cushions, toys
Armchair, *On it:* toys, tin of baby powder, towel
Sideboard. *On it:* toys, box of tissues, telephone, lamp
Coffee-table. *On it:* toy spade. *Under it:* "Mr Poddle"
Play-pen. *In it:* toys
Airing-rack. *On it:* various articles of children's clothing
On wall: child's painting
On floor: toys, bowl of unfolded nappies

Off stage: Glass of water (**Lucy**)
Toilet roll (**Lucy**)
Slip of paper (**Rosemary**)
Glass of orange juice (**Lucy**)
Plate of chocolate biscuits (**Lucy**)
Glass of milk (**Lucy**)

Personal: **Rosemary:** key on ring

(*Confusions.* London: French 1977, p. 61)

A relatively undemanding exercise to introduce inexperienced or unwilling students to the practical dimension of performing a play could be introduced along the following lines. Groups of students could study the text and put together property lists under the headings of:

- Things to eat.
- Furniture and household articles.
- Children's things.
- Sound effects.

The following is a slightly more demanding exercise for students with some knowledge of play analysis who are in a position to take a first step towards producing a play. The class can be asked to imagine that the property master is a particularly forgetful person. They must then consider which articles he could forget without damaging the production, and which are so essential that the play could not be performed satisfactorily without them. The discussion should lead to a focus on:

- the glass of water, milk and orange juice which are built into the dialogue and are directly linked with the central theme of the play;
- the telephone and door bells which mark stages in the progress of the scene.

Effects Plot

Cue 1	Lucy: "... leave Sarah alone." *Telephone rings*	(Page 9)
Cue 2	Lucy goes off to bedroom *Door chimes sound twice*	(Page 9)
Cue 3	Lucy: "That's for Jamie's toothipegs ..." *Door chimes sound*	(Page 9)
Cue 4	Lucy: "... smack your botty." *Back door bell rings twice*	(Page 9)
Cue 5	Lucy exits to kitchen *Pause, then door chimes sound twice*	(Page 13)
Cue 6	Lucy: "I'm coming ..." *Door chimes sound*	(Page 13)
Cue 7	Lucy: "Blooming kids. Honestly." *Telephone rings*	(Page 24)

(*Confusions*. London: French 1977, p. 67)

To help students realize that improvisation is essential if things go wrong during a production, they could adapt the conversation between Rosemary and Lucy on pages 10–12 in the Students' Book, as the actresses would have to if the door bell suddenly stopped working at the beginning of a performance.

If the class were sufficiently motivated to attempt their own production, the items on the property list should be familiar and easy to obtain. The positioning of the furniture on stage should also be discussed, taking into account that the actors must be able to move unhindered around the stage and that the audience's view of the action should not be impeded by clumsy positioning of stage props.

Discussing the Interview

"If an intelligent woman spends her days exclusively with children, she can very easily disappear."

A discussion of what Ayckbourn meant by this leads to a detailed study of the dialogue. Lucy has slipped into the role of a mother figure, and into the language register of her children. She is herself hardly aware of the fact. Her inability to see herself in any other capacity is reflected in her use of baby-talk on the one hand and her authoritative tone on the other. Her physical inability to escape from her situation is suggested by her costume (Details: Interview, p. 13–14: "*Mother Figure* – yes ... everything has been narrowed down to that.").

What does Lucy's way of speaking tell us about her character and views?

She speaks predominantly in one-word answers or statements at varying levels of command, showing her contempt for her visitors' childish behaviour and ideas. Only occasionally does she express an adult opinion in an adult way (Students' Book, p. 12: "I'm sorry ... my husband isn't home much" and p. 16: "That can apply to women, too, surely?"). Ayckbourn's comments are particularly useful in discussing this point (Interview, p. 19: "Yes, I'll tell you ... in half a sentence.").

Is there a turning point in character relationships?

Lucy's treatment of Terry is a revelation to Rosemary. "That's the way to talk to him." (Students' Book, p. 20, l. 7). It gives her a little more courage to assert herself, even though it only takes the childish form of sticking her tongue out. From this point on, Terry no longer behaves like a neighbour trying to humour a slightly eccentric woman, but also lapses into the role of a naughty child. From what he says in his interview, Alan Ayckbourn intended the "liberationist tract in Lucy" to be at least noticed by the audience. "One hopes that she has gone away with something new, so perhaps has Terry." (Interview, p.19).

Why is Terry so easily intimidated?

Terry's character demonstrates one of the "many facets of human behaviour" Ayckbourn hopes to present (Students' Book, p. 7). The class may need a little prompting from the teacher, however, before they can deal with this question for themselves. Ayckbourn's comments on the policewoman can be used as a lead-in to this question (Interview, pp. 18–19: "I was very amused ... what this woman does to Terry."). Ernest, in *A Talk in the Park*, is a similar type of character.

Suggesting Further Activities

Evaluation of stage directions

In most scripts, the stage directions are usually very sparse. Of course the dialogue also contains many clues which the actor must interpret and translate into actions, but a great deal is still left to the discretion of the director and the actors. This dimension is often overlooked until students are confronted with producing a play themselves. Students could try and put themselves in the position of the director. Before even beginning rehearsals, he has to be clear in his own mind about his interpretation of the play; what it is saying and how it is being said. He must then picture these ideas as actions on stage, perhaps in the form of detailed stage directions for each speech. Students could also try this exercise, imagining they are going to produce one of the many cameo episodes in the play.

Example: (Students' Book, p. 16)

Rosemary: "Very pleasant orange juice."
(sits uncomfortably on edge of seat – feet together – holds glass with both hands – sips gingerly at orange juice trying to give impression that she is enjoying the drink by smiling feebly.)

Lucy: "Full of vitamin C."
(stands erect over Rosemary with very self-satisfied look on her face – nod of the head to enforce truth of what she is saying.)

Terry: "No, I didn't want to give you the wrong impression there ..."
(has looked very sheepish up to now, realizing his blunder – lounges on sofa, legs crossed to give impression of ease and cover his embarrassment.)

Alternatively, students could write a description of an episode to someone who hadn't been able to see the play. This would also involve details of movements, attitudes, gestures and facial expressions.

Obviously, there is no right or wrong version for the students to aim at. What the play should look like in performance is very largely a matter of opinion. If the opportunity presents itself, students could extend this activity by talking over their ideas with an actor or actress to test if their theories would work in practice.

Integration of the play in a thematic unit

Mother Figure should be discussed in connection with other plays from *Confusions.* However, it could also be an integral part of a thematic unit on family life, specifically on the role of children in the life of their parents. Michael Frayn's *Black and Silver,* too, is a so-called one-act play, a two-hander on "domestic misadventures". The setting is a hotel bedroom in Venice. Husband and wife are asleep. At three o'clock in the morning their small baby starts first to fret and then to cry. As the wife is supposed to be having a holiday, her husband gets up to quiet the baby and tries to get him back to sleep again. This happens repeatedly during the night. Husband and wife discuss the change that has taken place in their life since the baby was born.

Another play about parenthood and married life is Ted Whitehead's *Alpha Beta,* a three-act play. But this is an attack on the traditional concept of marriage and family. It raises the question whether women should be conditioned to confine their aspiration to the role of wife/mother in the nuclear family. It suggests that children should be brought up in larger groupings.

Between Mouthfuls

A hotel dining-room

Two tables are set apart, each with two chairs. Between them a service table. An IN and OUT door from the kitchens. The main entrance for Guests. The discreet clatter of knives and forks from other invisible diners. The Waiter is finishing arranging his two tables. He wanders over and leans against the service table. At length, Donald Pearce enters, a middle-aged businessman. The waiter is humming to himself

PEARCE Waiter!

WAITER *(approaching him)* Good evening, sir.

PEARCE Good evening. I have a table for two reserved in the name of Pearce.

WAITER Table for two, sir. Did you make a reservation, sir?

PEARCE Yes, I've just said I did.

WAITER Very good, sir. *(He consults the reservations book on the service table)* What name was it, sir?

PEARCE Pearce. I've just this minute said so.

WAITER Pearce – with a P, I presume? – ah, yes, sir. *(Indicating the table nearer the door)* Would this one over here suit you, sir?

---

discreet [–'–] *here:* not loud
clatter rattling noise, as of a knife against a plate
to hum [hʌm] summen

PEARCE No, I don't think it would. I think I'd prefer this one over here.

WAITER Oh, just as you like, sir.

The Waiter leads Pearce over to the table and holds the chair for Pearce, who sits, his back to the rest of the room

WAITER Sir –

PEARCE Thank you.

WAITER Just yourself is it, sir?

PEARCE No.

WAITER Ah. Someone will be joining you, will they, sir?

PEARCE Yes, indeed. That's really rather why I reserved a table for two.

WAITER Right, sir.

The Waiter goes to the service table to collect menus

Emma Pearce enters, same age as Pearce, worried and tense. She catches sight of her husband and moves across to join him

MRS PEARCE *(distant)* Ah –

The Waiter hurries across to help her with her chair

PEARCE Oh, there you are.

WAITER Good evening, madam.

MRS PEARCE *(sitting)* Thank you. *(To Pearce)* You might have waited for me.

PEARCE I had absolutely no idea where you'd got to.

MRS PEARCE You know perfectly well where I was.

WAITER *(handing her a menu)* Thank you, madam.

MRS PEARCE I told you.

WAITER Thank you, sir.

PEARCE Thank you.

MRS PEARCE Oh lord. I suppose I've got to read through all this. *(She fumbles in her bag)*

WAITER Would you, madam, or yourself care for a drink before your meal, sir?

PEARCE No, we wouldn't, thank you.

MRS PEARCE Oh no, I haven't brought them.

---

to collect menus ['menju:z] to pick up menu cards to show them to the guests
tense not calm and relaxed
to fumble (in a bag) to put one's hand in a bag, looking for s.th.
would you care for ...? would you like ...?

PEARCE We may have some wine.
WAITER Right, sir.
MRS PEARCE That's that. I haven't brought them. *(She takes out a cigarette)*
PEARCE What?
MRS PEARCE My reading glasses. I've left them at home.
PEARCE I suppose that means I've got to read it to you.

The Waiter lights Mrs Pearce's cigarette

MRS PEARCE Unless you want me to guess.
PEARCE *(to the Waiter)* Would you bring us an ashtray, please.
WAITER Yes, sir.
PEARCE Why the hell you can't keep your glasses permanently in your handbag...

The Waiter moves away humming. As he does so, Pearce's voice fades out. Throughout we hear only that dialogue that the Waiter himself hears when within earshot. Whether or not the Waiter registers the content of what he is hearing apart from remarks directly addressed to him, he never betrays. Pearce continues speaking, but we can no longer hear him. The Waiter fetches the ashtray from the service table, dusts it, and returns to Pearce's table

MRS PEARCE *(fading up)* ... this afternoon whilst I was reading and I forgot them, that's all.
PEARCE All right, all right, all right.
MRS PEARCE *(to the Waiter)* Thank you.
PEARCE And we'll have the wine list as well.
WAITER Wine list. Yes, sir.
PEARCE Now then, are you listening? Here we go. *(Reading)* Hors d'œuvres from our trolley, grapefruit cocktail... *(He fades out)*

The Waiter returns to the service table for the wine list, humming

Polly and Martin enter, a younger couple

MARTIN Er. Waiter –

---

to fade out disappear slowly; to speak less and less loudly until one cannot be heard
within earshot near enough to hear what s.o. is saying
to dust to rub with a cloth to remove dust (Staub)
trolley table on wheels, used in restaurants

WAITER Good evening, sir. Good evening, madam. Just the two of you, is there?

MARTIN That's right.

WAITER Have you a reservation, sir?

MARTIN No, we haven't.

WAITER Just a moment, sir. *(He consults the book)*

POLLY I hope there's going to be room.

MARTIN *(looking round the restaurant)* There'll be room. *(Catching sight of the Pearces)* God, look who's here.

POLLY Where?

MARTIN Over there, look. Donald Pearce and his wife.

POLLY Oh.

MARTIN Better go and say hallo.

POLLY No, don't do that.

MARTIN What?

POLLY Let's go somewhere else.

MARTIN What?

POLLY They'll only feel they'll have to ask us to join them. Let's go somewhere else.

MARTIN I'm not going somewhere else.

POLLY They haven't seen us yet. Quick ...

MARTIN I'm not going somewhere else. What's the matter with you?

POLLY I just don't feel like talking to them.

MARTIN Why not?

POLLY Not now.

WAITER Sorry to keep you, sir. Would this table here be all right, sir?

MARTIN *(as they follow him to the other table)* You can't expect me to cut my boss dead in a restaurant.

POLLY We'll have to pretend we haven't seen them.

MARTIN It's obvious we've seen them.

POLLY Why? They haven't seen us. We could leave now.

The Waiter holds the chair for Polly

MARTIN I'm not leaving now. *(He sits. To the Waiter)* Thank you. *(To Polly)* What's got into you?

POLLY Nothing. *(She sits)*

WAITER Excuse me, sir.

MARTIN I mean, I thought you always got on with them.

---

to cut s.o. dead to ignore s.o., not to speak to s.o.

POLLY They're all right.

WAITER Excuse me, sir.

MARTIN You've always been quite happy to talk to them in the past.

WAITER Would you care for a drink before your meal, sir?

MARTIN You used to be perfectly happy ... *(To the Waiter)* No, thank you – perfectly happy to go round when they invited us.

POLLY Not tonight. I don't feel like sitting down ... *(She fades out)*

The Waiter returns to the service table and picks up the wine list. He moves to the Pearces' table with it, humming to himself

PEARCE *(fading up)* ... Dover sole meuniere. Lobster thermidor. Lobster americaine brackets when in season ...

WAITER Wine list, sir.

PEARCE ... Scampi – all sorts of scampi – grilled halibut ... *(He fades out)*

The Waiter has slipped the wine list down beside Pearce's elbow and departed, humming. He returns to his service table, takes up two menus and crosses to Martin's table

POLLY ... seen you for three weeks. I'd rather like if we were just on our own.

MARTIN I'm not the one who went away.

POLLY All the same ...

MARTIN I mean, you're the one who went off on holiday. I didn't go off on holiday.

WAITER Menu, madam.

POLLY You could have done. *(Taking her menu)* Thank you.

MARTIN I couldn't, I told you. Old Pearce there – *(taking his menu)* – thank you – old Pearce there landed me with enough work to last me a year.

POLLY That wasn't my fault, Martin ...

MARTIN I'm not saying it was. I was merely explaining why ...

---

sole meunière [mə'nɪeə] fried sole (Seezunge)
lobster Hummer; ~ thermidor: gekochtes Hummerfleisch mit Champignons, Eiern und Sherry
brackets *an expression printed in brackets looks like this:* (lobster americaine)
halibut ['hælɪbət] Heilbutt
all the same trotzdem
to land s.o. with work *(colloq.)* to give s.o. (a lot of) work to do

The Waiter departs humming. He edges towards the Pearces' table with his order pad

PEARCE ... grilled pork chops, tournedos à la Crowne – what ever that might be – steak diane, grilled fillet steak brackets when available. Rump steak – Garni ...

The Waiter withdraws humming to himself and leans against the service table, waiting. After a moment, he moves again to Martin's table to see if any decision has been made there

MARTIN ... book a holiday at a time when you know I'm going to be very busy.

POLLY Because if I waited for you not to be busy I'd never get a holiday at all.

MARTIN Come on, darling. This chap wants us to order.

WAITER Oh, no hurry, sir, no hurry.

POLLY I mean, it was either a case of my taking a holiday on my own or not having a ...

The Waiter wanders back to the Pearces, humming

PEARCE ... roast Aylesbury duckling with orange sauce. Roast spring chicken with stuffing. Roast turkey with cranberry sauce ...

The Waiter withdraws.

MARTIN *(very distant)* Waiter –

The Waiter moves to Martin's table

POLLY ... enjoy going on holiday on my own.

MARTIN Waiter, what's the Soup of the Day?

WAITER *(checking over Martin's shoulder)* Er – minestrone, sir.

MARTIN *(unenthusiastically)* Oh.

---

to edge to move very slowly
tournedos ['tʊənədəʊ] small fillet of beef with a strip of fat round it
steak diane [daɪ'æn] thinly-cut rump steak, fried quickly on both sides, and served in a sauce made of cream, onions and red wine
to withdraw to go back
Aylesbury ['eɪlzbərɪ] **duckling** young duck from Aylesbury (a country town north-west of London, famous for its ducks)
stuffing Füllung
cranberry Preiselbeere

Martin and Polly ponder their menus. The Waiter hovers

How was the trip back?

POLLY Not bad. Had to be at the airport at seven this morning. We got to Heathrow at ten …

MARTIN Sorry I couldn't meet you.

POLLY I didn't expect you to.

MARTIN Our sales meeting went on till lunchtime.

Pearce signals and mimes Waiter

WAITER Yes, sir?

The Waiter moves across from Martin's table to Pearce's

PEARCE Waiter, what is the Soup of the Day?

WAITER Minestrone, sir.

PEARCE Oh.

Pause

WAITER Do you wish to order now, sir?

MRS PEARCE Do you do Eggs Benedict?

WAITER *(doubtfully; looking over Pearce's shoulder)* Eggs Benedict, madam …

PEARCE I should imagine that if they did Eggs Benedict, they'd have put Eggs Benedict on the menu.

WAITER I don't think we do, madam.

MRS PEARCE I was only asking.

PEARCE I mean, I read you the menu very distinctly. I didn't read out Eggs Benedict, did I?

MRS PEARCE I don't know.

PEARCE But I've only just this minute finished reading it to you.

MRS PEARCE I don't know, I wasn't listening.

PEARCE *(taking a deep breath)* I think we need a few more minutes to decide, Waiter.

WAITER Very good, sir.

PEARCE I suppose you want me to read it to you all over again …

---

to hover ['hɒvə] to stand, waiting for s.th.
Heathrow name of London airport
to mime to make signs with the hands, without speaking
Eggs Benedict ['benɪdɪkt] poached eggs (verlorene Eier) on a slice of tongue, served with sauce mornay (cheese sauce)

The Waiter hovers back near Martin and Polly

POLLY ... marvellous the whole time. Baking hot. And it's a beautiful island.

MARTIN *(uninterestedly)* Yes. Sounds it. *(Seeing the Waiter)* Ah. Now then. So far we've got one pâté – one smoked trout. And you were ...?

WAITER *(writing)* Pâté maison – smoked trout.

POLLY Is the lobster fresh?

WAITER Oh yes, madam. I can recommend it.

POLLY Then I'll have Thermidor with a green salad.

MARTIN Poulet estragon for me.

WAITER Poulet estragon – thermidor. Would you care to see the wine list, sir?

MARTIN Might as well. My wife has just returned from the sunny Mediterranean. She's probably got the taste after three weeks.

WAITER Very nice, too, madam. Excuse me a moment, sir.

The Waiter moves across again to the Pearces

MRS PEARCE ... the moment you come back, you start.

PEARCE I'm not starting again. I was merely saying ... *(Seeing the Waiter)* Yes?

WAITER I just wondered if you were ready with your order yet, sir.

PEARCE No indeed, we are not ready with our order yet. We will let you know when we are.

WAITER Very good, sir.

MRS PEARCE Every single time you come back from somewhere, you're absolutely ...

The Waiter collects the wine list from the service table

MARTIN ... it was your idea.

POLLY I didn't know they were going to be here, did I?

MARTIN It was your idea we came out.

POLLY Since the children were away, I thought it would be nice.

MARTIN It was a lovely idea. Enjoy it.

POLLY Yes, but I didn't know they were going to be here, did I ...

PEARCE *(calling)* Waiter!

---

baking hot very hot
pâté ['pæteɪ] paste made of meat, liver, etc., eaten cold
trout Forelle
poulet chicken
might as well yes, please *(not very enthusiastic)*

The Waiter returns to Pearce

WAITER Sir?

PEARCE You will be pleased to hear that we have at last decided. Pencil at the ready. Here we go. One potted shrimps – one grapefruit cocktail and if it has a maraschino cherry on it, we don't want it. One Dover sole meuniere off the bone – one rump steak, just this side of medium rare ...

WAITER *(scribbling furiously)* Just a minute, sir – Dover sole off the bone – rump steak, medium rare ... Have you decided on a wine, sir?

PEARCE Oh – yes. *(He opens the list)* White? Emma? White, do you want white?

MRS PEARCE I don't mind either way. I only want half a glass.

PEARCE Well, just say red or white?

MRS PEARCE I honestly don't mind. *(She looks out front)*

PEARCE Red, then.

Mrs Pearce turns sharply and glares at him

Ah, now. What have you got in the Italian line?

WAITER I think they're at the back here, sir. The wine waiter's not on at the moment, otherwise ...

PEARCE Ah yes, here we are, Italian. We had a very very reasonable one at the hotel where we stayed.

MRS PEARCE I thought you went there to work.

PEARCE I did go there to work. I had to stop occasionally. Now then.

MRS PEARCE My husband's been overworking in Italy, poor thing ...

PEARCE No, you don't seem to have it.

MRS PEARCE I don't know how you managed to work in all that blazing sunshine.

PEARCE A bottle of this one here, the – er – one-oh-four.

WAITER Oh right, sir. The – er – one-oh-four. Yes, sir.

MRS PEARCE How on earth did you manage to cope for three whole weeks ...?

---

pencil at the ready *(colloq.)* pencil in the hand, ready to write
shrimp Krabbe
potted shrimps preserved shrimps; konservierte Krabben
the wine waiter's not on the waiter who takes orders for wine is not here
very reasonable quite good and not too expensive
one-oh-four 104; the number of the wine on the wine list
to cope to manage

The Waiter goes out through to the kitchens and after a second, returns. He takes up some cutlery, places it on a tray and crosses to Martin's table

MARTIN ... last six months are beginning to move. Somebody up there seems to have our interests at heart, anyway.

WAITER Smoked trout, madam?

MARTIN No, that's me – and not before time, as far as I'm concerned. Old Pearce was back this afternoon, full of the joys of spring, anyway. I don't know what he got up to in Rome but he seems to have had a good time of it.

The Waiter exchanges some of Polly's and Martin's cutlery, replacing it with a fish knife and fork

WAITER Excuse me, madam.

POLLY I thought he went on business.

MARTIN I can't believe it took him three weeks to get a contract signed. I know the Italians are difficult ... mind you, I think if I was married to Emma Pearce, I'd chase off to Rome.

POLLY Don't stare.

MARTIN It's all right, he's got his back to us. And she's as blind as a bat. No, he probably had some little Italian señora lined up there. He always likes to mix his business with a bit of ...

The Waiter goes to Pearce's table

WAITER Potted shrimps, sir?

PEARCE Thank you.

WAITER And a steak for madam?

PEARCE No, that's for me as well.

A pause while the Waiter exchanges cutlery, replacing Mrs Pearce's with a fish knife and fork, and Pearce's with an outer fish knife and fork and a steak knife

MRS PEARCE Well, I'm sorry, I don't believe you.

PEARCE That's up to you. *(Pause)* That's what I was doing.

MRS PEARCE I'm sorry, I think you're a liar.

---

cutlery knives, forks, spoons, etc.
not before time *(colloq.)* nearly late
as blind as a bat quite blind (bat: Fledermaus)
outer fish knife fish knife next to a meat knife, further from the plate

The Waiter crosses to Martin and Polly

MARTIN ... and the problem was to re-allocate staff work schedules so that everyone was guaranteed at least one day off in three whilst guaranteeing normal production.

POLLY Yes.

WAITER Excuse me, sir.

MARTIN Which was one hell of a problem. Yes?

WAITER Have you chosen a wine, sir?

MARTIN *(picking up the wine list)* Oh yes – you see, as soon as you say, lost men off the assembly section, you had to ensure you had sufficient manpower to tide you over the entire three-day period without any noticeable shrinkage in labour effectiveness.

POLLY Martin, he's waiting to know what wine.

MARTIN Oh yes. Do you do a carafe?

WAITER Yes, sir.

MARTIN A carafe of white. Not too sweet.

WAITER Carafe of the white, sir.

MARTIN Anyway, we managed it. We put in the report and Donald Pearce is over the moon. I mean, he only had time to glance at it this afternoon but ...

The Waiter goes into the kitchens

The Pearces sit in silence. Martin chatters on to Polly

The Waiter returns with the Pearces' first courses, grapefruit cocktail, potted shrimps, plate of toast. He crosses to Pearce's table

WAITER Grapefruit cocktail, madam?

MRS PEARCE Thank you.

WAITER Potted shrimps, sir.

PEARCE Thank you.

---

to re-allocate staff work schedules to re-organize the work of people at the office
assembly section workers on the assembly line (Fließband)
shrinkage becoming less or smaller
do you do ...? can you serve us with ...?
carafe [kə'ræf] Karaffe
to be over the moon *(colloq.)* to be very happy
to chatter on to go on talking

MRS PEARCE I'm sorry, I think you're lying.

WAITER Beg your pardon, madam? Oh, I'm sorry, madam, I beg your pardon. Toast is there, sir.

The Waiter returns to the kitchens, humming to himself

The Pearces eat, Martin continues to talk

The Waiter returns with Martin's and Polly's first courses. He goes to their table

MARTIN ... so in the end I did the only thing possible. I took on entire responsibility for the whole A, D and J project. Took on both jobs. Did the lot myself.

POLLY Yes, I know, you told me this before, Martin.

The Waiter serves her with pâté

Thank you.

MARTIN When did I tell you? *(He leans forward over the table)*

The Waiter tries unsuccessfully to slip the plate under Martin's hands

POLLY I've only been away three weeks, you know.

MARTIN What time are we picking up the kids?

POLLY I told Gran we'd be there in time for lunch.

MARTIN Ah well, end of peace and quiet. *(He leans back)*

The Waiter quickly slides Martin's plate into place

Thank you.

POLLY Did you miss them?

MARTIN I honestly haven't had a moment to miss anyone, love. Not even you.

POLLY I missed them dreadfully.

WAITER *(fiddling at the table)* Toast is just there, madam.

POLLY Thank you.

MARTIN Oh, did I tell you, Graham Shotter finally got that job in Glasgow.

POLLY Oh, did he ...

A, D and J project the letters stand for an important plan within the firm
Gran Grandmother
fiddling *here:* waiting impatiently

The Waiter goes to the kitchen, returning with both the carafe and Pearce's wine. He puts the carafe down on the service table, wipes the bottle, shakes it upside down, then takes it to Pearce's table and holds it out for his inspection

WAITER Sir. The one-oh-four, sir.

PEARCE Oh yes. *(He reads the label very carefully, muttering all the words to himself including the name of the shippers)* Righto, yes.

WAITER Thank you, sir.

The Waiter produces a cork-screw from his pocket and starts to open the bottle by their table

PEARCE Did you get someone in to look at that radiator in the bedroom?

MRS PEARCE They said they'd come on Tuesday.

PEARCE Oh.

MRS PEARCE He said it sounded as if it needed a new part.

PEARCE That's out.

The Waiter pulls out the cork with a "pop"

I'm not paying for a new part. I'm not wasting money on that.

MRS PEARCE Just on holidays. *(She lights another cigarette)*

The Waiter pours a little wine into Pearce's glass

PEARCE Are you deliberately trying to annoy me this evening?

WAITER Would you care to try it, sir?

PEARCE Oh ... *(He sips his glass)* Bit on the chill side. It'll do. Go ahead.

WAITER Thank you, sir.

The Waiter starts to pour wine for Mrs Pearce

MRS PEARCE That's enough, thank you.

WAITER Thank you, madam.

PEARCE Are you eating that or just leaving it?

MRS PEARCE Leaving it.

The Waiter pours Pearce the rest of his glass and puts the bottle on the table

---

shippers the firm which imported the wine
bit on the chill side slightly cold

WAITER I'll leave it here, sir. Finished, madam?

MRS PEARCE Yes, thank you.

WAITER Was it all right for you, madam?

MRS PEARCE Beautiful. I'm just not very hungry.

WAITER *(removing her plate)* Thank you, madam.

PEARCE I don't see any point in ordering food if you're not going to eat it …

The Waiter returns to the service table, picks up the carafe of wine and crosses to Martin and Polly's table

POLLY I just think it's a terrific cheek, that's all.

MARTIN No, honestly, love, it isn't really I – thank you – just pour it –

WAITER Sir.

The Waiter starts to pour wine for Polly. She picks up her glass while he is still pouring

MARTIN The quality of the wife is frightfully important. If you've got a top executive virtually responsible for what? – two or three hundred men sometimes – it's vitally important that he's married to the right woman.

POLLY Why?

MARTIN Well, that he has a stable relationship. That she's suddenly not going to walk out on him.

The Waiter picks up Martin's glass and fills it, so that Martin cannot touch it until he has finished pouring

POLLY She's going to take no part in his work, is she?

MARTIN Well, hardly, no.

POLLY Then I think the firm ought to mind its own bloody business, I'm sorry …

The Waiter moves away, humming. Pearce finishes. The Waiter moves in to take his plate

MRS PEARCE I said, who is she?

PEARCE Who is who?

MRS PEARCE Who is she?

---

a terrific cheek *(colloq.)* eine verdammte Frechheit
virtually [ˈvɜːtʃʊəlɪ] more or less
to walk out on s.o. to go away and leave s.o.

Pearce opens his mouth to reply then becomes aware of the waiter. The Waiter takes away his plate and puts it on the service table. He sees Polly and Martin have finished and goes to remove their plates

POLLY … what I'm saying is, that as far as I'm concerned, you could be manufacturing – marmalade. You spend all day in the office, you work at home most of the night, you never talk to the children and I don't even know half the time what it is that you're doing.

MARTIN Look, darling, you wouldn't understand if I told you …

The Waiter takes the empty plates to the kitchen

Pearce and Mrs Pearce are having a short, terse conversation. Martin talks agitatedly. Polly looks slightly desperate

The Waiter returns with the Pearces' second course: rump steak for him, Dover sole for her, and vegetables. He goes to their table

PEARCE I don't think this is quite the occasion for this sort of conversation, do you?

MRS PEARCE I can't think of any better time.

PEARCE In a public restaurant.

MRS PEARCE Why not?

WAITER Dover sole, madam.

MRS PEARCE Thank you.

PEARCE I don't see any point in causing a scene …

MRS PEARCE I am not causing a scene. I asked you a perfectly normal question. Who is this woman?

WAITER Rump steak, sir.

PEARCE What does it matter?

MRS PEARCE Because I want to know.

PEARCE Who said there was anyone, anyway?

MRS PEARCE Oh, come along, darling, I am not a fool. I am not a bloody fool.

PEARCE Would you mind lowering your voice.

MRS PEARCE I will not lower my voice.

WAITER Runner beans, madam?

---

terse [tɜːs] in few words
agitated ['ædʒɪteɪtɪd] excited
runner beans grüne Bohnen

MRS PEARCE No, thank you.

WAITER Carrots, madam?

MRS PEARCE No, thank you. I want nothing else.

WAITER No potatoes either, madam?

MRS PEARCE *(shrilly)* Nothing else.

WAITER Very good, madam. *(He moves round to Pearce)*

PEARCE *(to Mrs Pearce, fiercely)* Could you kindly try and control yourself.

WAITER Runner beans for you, sir?

PEARCE *(snarling at him)* Yes please.

MRS PEARCE Well, I'll tell you one thing, darling, if I ever get my hands on the little whore, I'll wring her neck.

PEARCE Do you mind, do you mind.

WAITER Carrots, sir?

PEARCE Yes.

MRS PEARCE You can tell the little bitch that from me.

WAITER Potatoes, sir?

PEARCE No. No potatoes. Nothing else.

WAITER Very good, sir.

PEARCE Nothing else, at all.

WAITER Right, sir.

The Waiter moves away and returns to the kitchens

Both tables are in a fair state of animation

The Waiter returns with Polly's and Martin's main courses: lobster, chicken, salad dressing, salad, vegetables. He moves to their table

POLLY ... that's what it boils down to. I'm not in the slightest bit interested in your work and you don't give a damn what I'm up to. There we are. We haven't one thing in common.

---

to snarl to speak in a very unfriendly way
whore [hɔ:] prostitute
to wring s. o.'s neck to kill s.o. by strangling
do you mind be careful
bitch female dog; *here:* used to describe a woman that one does not like
fair state of animation rather excited
that's what it boils down to *(colloq.)* darauf läuft es hinaus
what I'm up to what I do

MARTIN Oh, come on, I don't know.

The Waiter serves Polly's lobster

POLLY Thank you.

MARTIN I'm interested in what you're up to.

POLLY Really?

MARTIN Of course ...

POLLY Nonsense.

MARTIN It's not nonsense at all.

WAITER *(serving)* Poulet estragon, sir.

POLLY These last three weeks I was away, were you the slightest bit interested in where I was?

MARTIN I know where you were.

POLLY Do you?

MARTIN You were in – wherever it is – Majorca.

POLLY I was not in Majorca, darling, as it happens. I was in Rome.

WAITER Vegetables, sir?

MARTIN Er – just carrots. Rome? What were you doing in Rome?

POLLY I was with Donald Pearce.

MARTIN Donald Pearce – that's fine, thank you – what were you doing with Donald Pearce?

POLLY I spent three weeks with Donald Pearce in a hotel in Rome.

MARTIN My God. *(He puts his head in his hands on the table)*

WAITER Potatoes, sir?

MARTIN Oh my God.

WAITER *(bending right down to speak to Martin)* Excuse me, sir.

POLLY *(to the Waiter)* No, he doesn't.

WAITER Oh, right, madam.

POLLY *(to Martin)* I'm sorry.

WAITER Sorry, madam?

POLLY Nothing.

WAITER Oh, sorry, madam. Green salad.

MARTIN Oh my God.

POLLY Thank you.

WAITER French dressing, madam?

POLLY Yes, just a little.

MARTIN How could you do it?

POLLY I don't know. I'm sorry. I felt – I don't know ...

MARTIN You realize what you've done?

POLLY It's not important, darling, it's all over. That's why I told you.

MARTIN It may be all over for you. What happens when she finds out?

POLLY Who?

MARTIN Emma Pearce. You realize what's going to happen to me.

POLLY What?

MARTIN I'll be out on my ear. As soon as Emma Pearce gets wind of – oh, damn it. If you were going to choose someone why the hell did it have to be Donald Pearce? That's it, don't you see? That's the end of everything. The end of my prospects of promotion. I shall probably be forced to resign.

POLLY Is that what's worrying you?

MARTIN Of course it's what's worrying me.

WAITER Is that sufficient for you, madam?

POLLY Oh, for crying out loud, I can't believe it – I just can't believe it. *(She stands, pushing back her chair)*

MARTIN Where are you going?

POLLY Don't you care anything for me? Nothing at all?

MARTIN Where are you going?

POLLY I'm going to be physically sick.

Polly storms out

WAITER Was everything all right for madam, sir?

MARTIN Yes, it was fine, fine. Thank you very much.

WAITER Thank you, sir.

The Waiter moves away and crosses to the Pearces' table with the intention of topping up the wine glasses, trying not to be noticed

PEARCE For the last time, will you pull yourself together.

MRS PEARCE I'll kill her when I see her, I'll kill her.

PEARCE Don't be so stupid. *(Seeing the Waiter, sharply)* What do you want, Waiter?

WAITER I was – just going to pour some more wine, sir.

PEARCE We can do that ourselves. Go away.

WAITER Just as you like, sir. *(He starts to go)*

---

out on one's ear thrown out

prospects of promotion chances of getting a better job in the firm

to be physically sick to bring back (throw up) what one has eaten (erbrechen)

to top up *(colloq.)* to fill up

MRS PEARCE Waiter.

WAITER Madam?

MRS PEARCE *(indicating her plate)* You can take this away.

WAITER Have you finished, madam?

MRS PEARCE Yes, it was quite delicious, thank you very much. *(She gets up)* Excuse me.

WAITER Was everything all right, madam?

MRS PEARCE Perfectly. It's just I'm afraid I'm unable to enjoy a meal with a man who turns out to be a deceitful, lecherous liar.

Mrs Pearce flips Pearce's plate into his lap. Pearce leaps up

Mrs Pearce goes out of the restaurant hurriedly, blowing her nose. She passes by Martin without seeing him.

Martin, sitting stunned, does not see her

PEARCE *(dabbing at his trousers with his napkin)* Oh, for the love of mike.

WAITER I'll get a cloth, sir. Just a minute.

PEARCE Look at this, look at these trousers. Where's the Gents? I'll have to mop up.

Martin rises.

WAITER Just through here, sir. I'll show you.

The Waiter leads Pearce to the door past Martin's table. Martin has risen

PEARCE Damn fool thing to do. What a damn … *(He bumps into Martin)* Oh – excuse me, I – good God, hallo, Chalmers.

MARTIN Oh, hallo, Mr Pearce.

---

deceitful [dɪ'si:tfʊl] not telling the truth
lecherous ['letʃərəs] lüstern
to flip to turn over
stunned benommen
to dab to touch (with a cloth)
napkin *here:* Serviette
for the love of mike *(more common:* for Pete's sake) for God's sake
Gents men's toilet

PEARCE I didn't know you were here. Excuse me, I've just had a bit of a mishap.

MARTIN Oh, good heavens, yes.

PEARCE Having a night out, are you?

MARTIN Yes, yes, that's right.

PEARCE So are we. Well, have to unwind once in a while, don't you?

MARTIN Rather, rather ...

PEARCE Are you still eating, or are you ...?

MARTIN No, I was just ...

PEARCE Well, I'll tell you what. I've just go to have a quick mop up in the Gents. Won't be a second. Then – fancy a quick brandy in the bar?

MARTIN Well, that would be very nice indeed, Mr Pearce.

PEARCE Just a quick one ... *(To the Waiter, who is still mopping at his trouser)* All right, that'll do, Waiter, thank you. Could you bring the bill through to the bar, please.

WAITER Yes, of course, sir.

PEARCE Oh, and you can put them all on to one if you like.

MARTIN Oh, that's most generous of you, sir.

PEARCE Not at all, not at all. I think after all that stalwart work you've done on that report I probably owe you a meal, don't I?

MARTIN Oh, I don't know about that ...

The Waiter moves out of earshot. Pearce claps Martin on the back. The Waiter starts to clear the Pearces' table

Pearce and Martin leave the restaurant, Pearce with his hand on Martin's shoulder, both laughing and talking animatedly

The Waiter looks out front, as –

the CURTAIN *falls*

---

mishap accident
to unwind to relax, to become less excited and nervous
to have a mop up *(colloq.) here:* to dry oneself
put them all on to one *(colloq.)* I will pay both bills
stalwart ['stɔ:lwət] handfest
animated excited and happy

Introducing the Play

Donald Pearce, a middle-aged businessman and his wife are having dinner in a hotel dining room. Mr Pearce, just returned from a business trip in Rome, is rather curt, impatient and irritated both with his wife and the attending waiter. While Mr Pearce is reading out the menu to his wife – who has incidentally left her reading glasses at home – Polly and Martin, a young couple, enter the dining room. Martin is an employee at Mr Pearce's firm, and on seeing the Pearces Martin feels immediately obliged to go and greet them. On Polly's entreating, however, he refrains from doing so although his wife's reaction is incomprehensible to him. Polly has been on holiday alone for the past three weeks because her husband had an exceedingly heavy work load and could not take time off. Martin's conversation revolves around his work and many oblique references are made to his boss's affinity for female company and to his rather good humour since his return from Rome. At the other table conversation is rather strained between the Pearces. Mrs Pearce appears to be rather indifferent not only to the courses on the menu but also to her husbund. She hints that Mr Pearce was not simply working in Italy and later on accuses him openly of infidelity. She demands to know who the lady in question is. In the meantime at the other table things have been coming to a head. Martin has been discussing his work und referring to the fact that the wife is important in the career of an executive, a stable relationship being the key to success. This statement and Martin's sole absorption in his job sparks off Polly's ensuing outburst. She accuses Martin of devoting himself entirely to his work and subsequently neglecting his children. She adds that they haven't anything in common any more and divulges then that she was in Rome with her husband's boss for the past three weeks. Martin is shocked at this revelation, not so much because of his wife's infidelity but because of the impending hazards to his career. Polly leaves the restaurant in disgust. At the other table tension has been rising and Mrs Pearce threatens to kill Mr Pearce's lady acquaintance. She tells the waiter that her husband is a deceitful and lecherous liar. Before leaving the restaurant she flips her husband's plate into his lap. In the end the two men have a brandy together in the bar. They appear to be very amiable to each other.

Analysing the Text

THEMES – STATEMENTS – QUESTIONS – QUOTATIONS

Suggestions and guidelines which can be used as starting points for classroom work and discussion. First numbers refer to the pages in the Students' Book, numbers in brackets refer to the lines.

Comedy, character studies and lack of communication

- between Mr Pearce and the waiter ▷ 26 (10)
  "That's really rather why I reserved a table for two."
- between Mr Pearce and his wife ▷ 31 (27)
  "I don't know, I wasn't listening."
- between Martin and Polly ▷ 36 (11)
  "Yes, I know, you told me this before, Martin."
- between the couples and the waiter when he is serving the meal ▷ 42 (12–13)
  Waiter: "Is that sufficient for you, madam?"
  Polly: "Oh, for crying out loud ..."
- semblance of communication between Mr Pearce and Martin ▷ 44 (11)
  "Then – fancy a quick brandy in the bar?"

Discussion prompt:
For what purposes does Ayckbourn use precise character study?

Husband and wife relationships

- Mr Pearce – middle-aged businessman with a "roving" spirit – successful – philandering – impatient, impolite and deceitful in dealings with his wife
- Mrs Pearce – realistic assessment of her marriage – no illusions about her husband – outspoken disgust
- Martin – assesses a wife in business terms
- Polly – feels neglected – admits the sterility of her relationship with her husband

Discussion prompt:
"You're a misery to live with these days, you really are." ▷ 18 (6)

Does Rosemary's comment in *Mother Figure* have any relevance to the situation in *Between Mouthfuls*?

Judging from the text, what is your impression of the two couples in *Between Mouthfuls*? Quote the passages which have led you to form your opinion.

The women versus the men

- By the end of the play the women are being presented as frank, honest – victims of their relationship with the men.
- By the end of the play the men are being portrayed as hypocritical, selfish, shallow.

Discussion prompt:
Polly and Mrs Pearce are both neglected by their husbands. Is this the only characteristic they have in common? Is Polly a younger generation Mrs Pearce, or has she characteristics which Mrs Pearce does not possess?

Sacrifice of personal life to ambition

- Martin has no time for holidays ▷ 30 (11)
- he has no real interest in his wife and family ▷ 31 (5), 36 (11), 39 (5–7), 40 (27)
- he is preoccupied with his work ▷ 34 (4), 35 (1–12), 36 (8–28)
- he attaches great importance to the social facade ▷ 28 (28), 38 (15), 42 (1–10), 44 (1–25)

Discussion prompt:
Which details does Ayckbourn use to present Martin as an ambitious young man? Quote the passages you think best illustrate this.

The "boss" and his image

- "I did go there to work. I had to stop occasionally." } ▷ 33 (23–24)
- "My husband's been overworking in Italy, poor thing." }
- "I can't believe it took him three weeks to get a contract signed." ▷ 34 (15)

Discussion prompt:
What impression is given of Mr Pearce in the text? Does Ayckbourn make any further use of the idea of the man seeing himself as the "boss" in any of the other plays?

The ritual of dining out

- In this play, as often in reality, the ritual of dining out is used to paper over the cracks. It is a mockery, a show put on to hide the breakdown of any meaningful relationship, in which impatience and distrust crack the veneer of social respectability.

Discussion prompt:
What do we learn about Mr and Mrs Pearce from their choice of expression on entering the restaurant?

The menu: clues to social standing, character and setting

- Soup of the Day is Minestrone (rather thin, weak and uninteresting, rather like the everyday life between the partners)
- Potted shrimps and rumpsteak "just this side of medium rare" (for Mr Pearce – expensive conservative choice – traditionally a man's dish)
- Grapefruit cocktail and Dover Sole (for Mrs Pearce – a little sour and colourless without the cherry – fish rather pale and insipid – not the sort of fish you would expect to find in a fish and chip shop – expensive, conservative choice – traditionally a woman's dish)
- Lobster with green salad (for Polly – expensive, exclusive, slightly daring and colourful choice – a dish for younger well-off palates)

- Poulet Estragon (for Martin – slightly out of the ordinary but basically mundane and uninteresting – the name gives the dish its social prestige)
- both couples drink wine (a sign of a middle-class restaurant – beer would not be an appropriate drink here)

Discussion prompt:
Ayckbourn makes the conversation about food form part of the comedy. For example Mr Pearce has to read the menu to his wife who does not bother to listen. Is this the only use Ayckbourn makes of this topic?

Farce and the absurd situation

– Mrs Pearce:	I'm sorry, I think you're lying.	
– Waiter:	Beg your pardon, madam? Oh, I'm sorry, madam, I beg your pardon. Toast is there, sir.	▷ 36 (1–3)
– See also	pp. 39–42, Students' Book	

Discussion prompt:
The banalities of serving food to the couples counterpoint their domestic upheavals, add to the comedy of the situation, and gently steer the action into the realm of farce. Find two examples of this in the play (See "Comedy and Farce").

The stage directions and the waiter

– The waiter is humming to himself.	▷ 27 (14), 38 (28)
– The waiter locks out front, as – the CURTAIN falls	▷ 44 (26)

Discussion prompt:
Stage directions give actors indications of how they should play a part at any one moment. The actor playing the part of the waiter in *Between Mouthfuls* knows that he must hum to himself while he is serving and perform a kind of juggling act with the plates and cutlery. Are these stage directions only necessary to help the actor raise a laugh, or do they also help the reader towards a better understanding of the ideas presented in the play? (See Interview)

Presenting the Cassette

Do social and regional accents play any role in the play?

It is important for actors and students to understand that the social standing of the characters is central to the action and implications of the play. The situation the characters find themselves in is "middle-class", and their escapades are traditionally "middle-class". The students might want to choose examples of similar German social behaviour and their corresponding speech habits and compare them with their English equivalents on the Cassette.

"Fading up" and "Fading out"

These techniques should not be unfamiliar to students who watch television. They may not, however, immediately recognize them on the printed page. Groups of students could prepare a sequence for reading or recording and then compare their ideas with the Cassette. Pages 32–33 in the Students' Book are particularly suitable for this kind of exercise. There is an additional "spin-off" advantage to this exercise. Students will soon realize that a technique which they have taken for granted is, in fact, very sophisticated, demanding a high level of acting and technical skill. This realization may well prompt them to view their television programmes with a more critical and appreciative eye.

"What makes a situation comic on stage?"

Pearce: I don't think this is quite the occasion ...
Waiter: Right, sir.
(Students' Book, pp. 39–40)

This particular passage, indeed almost the whole play when only read, might be interpreted as a pathetic, even tragic episode. On the Cassette it is presented as comedy, verging on farce. Students can discover for themselves what produces this comic effect. One group of students could prepare the above passage for presentation in a tragic form, another group for presentation as farce. When the versions are compared with each other and with the Cassette, it should become clear that not only the playwright – through his text and stage directions – but also the actors, through their interpretation, contribute to the effect produced. Our laughter depends to a great extent on the choice of intonation, stress, tone of voice, and pacing of speech and pauses. The play seen in production can vary considerably, depending on how these elements are dealt with.

How does the play end?

The social criticism implied in the ending of *Between Mouthfuls* is lightly handled and could easily be swamped by the comedy of the situation. It is therefore important to arouse students' curiosity in advance so that they direct their attention to it.

Before reading the play, a short synopsis of the plot could be given, ending along the following lines:

> The boss, Mr Pearce, leaves the room and notices
> the young executive, Mr Chalmers, for the first
> time and then ... What do you think happens?

Alternatively, a reading of the play could be cut short and students asked for their suggestions for an ending.

In either case, the Cassette can be used to put an end to speculation, and would be certain of very attentive listeners.

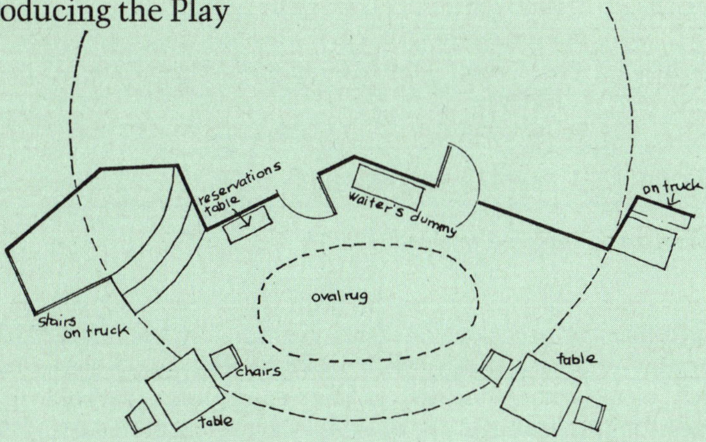

Between Mouthfuls

On stage: 4 chairs

2 tables. *On each:* 1 white cloth, 2 knives, 2 forks, 2 side plates with knives, 2 wine glasses, 2 napkins, 1 vase with flowers, cruet, book, matches, butter dish with butter

Waiter's dummy (serving-table). *On it:* 4 menus, 2 wine lists, 2 ashtrays, corkscrew, white cloth, tray with cutlery, steak knife, 4 fish knives and forks

Reservation table. *On it:* reservation book

Off stage: First Course: **(Waiter)**

1 grapefruit cocktail on small plate, spoon
1 potted shrimps, toast wrapped in napkin
1 liver pâté
1 trout
1 bottle of red wine
1 carafe of white wine

Second Course: **(Waiter)**

1 steak
1 Dover sole
1 vegetable dish with spoons – runner beans, carrots, potatoes
Lobster
Chicken
1 vegetable dish as above

Personal: **Waiter:** pad, pencil, corkscrew, lighter
Martin: cigarettes in case
Mrs Pearce: cigarettes in case, lighter in handbag
Polly: handbag

(*Confusions.* London: French 1977, pp. 62–63)

"We used a simplified version"

From a technical point of view this play is more demanding and complicated than the other two. Students might find it less intimidating if they are presented with Ayckbourn's comment quoted above (Interview, p. 16) at the same time as the property lists. They may find it interesting to speculate on what Ayckbourn left out and why. The students should soon begin to realize that the stage presentation is a major factor in determining the impact and interpretation of a play (Details: Interview, pp. 16–17, "When I staged it ...").

Blackboard:

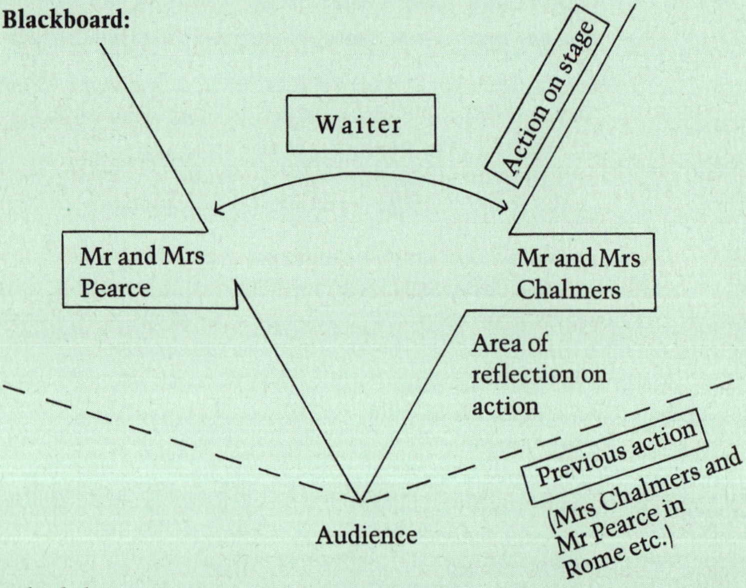

Which lines represent the action of the play? The waiter and what he hears or the area including what we learn about the characters and what has happened to them before they came on stage?

Discussing the Interview

Is the twist in the plot at the end of the play plausible, or just a dramatic device to provoke laughter?

This is an important point for the actors to decide in advance. They have to analyse the play just as carefully as any school class, perhaps more so, since their decision will determine their portrayal of the characters on stage, and directly influence the audience's reaction to the play.

Ayckbourn is clearly very aware of the implications of social standing (Students' Book, pp. 55–56). So it is safe to assume that his choice of characters is not accidental. The traditional view of middle-class morality they embody enables them to keep up the facade and accept the unacceptable with good grace, providing there is something to be gained (Interview, p. 20–21: "How would you comment ... I'm happy being a waiter.").

Would it be possible to adapt *Between Mouthfuls* as a radio or television play?

As Ayckbourn points out in his interview, *Between Mouthfuls* was originally written for television (Interview, p. 15: "The third play ... conversation and moving away). In the television version, the camera was the waiter and the microphone followed the waiter's movements. The convention of "fading", as is evident from the Cassette, is also effective for a radio production. Detailed clues to character and situation are embedded in the dialogue so that visual prompts are not absolutely necessary.

Is *Between Mouthfuls* a difficult play for an actor to interpret?

If this were a single one-act play, it would be difficult to categorize. On a first reading it seems very naturalistic, yet the situation contains elements of farce. The waiter is the pivot between these two positions. The impact of the play depends on the production. The setting, if too naturalistic, would detract from the fun of the farce, and as far as the characters are concerned the waiter is just part of the setting. The audience must depend on him to give them the right clues. Ayckbourn clearly sees him in the tradition of the Comedia dell' Arte (Interview, p. 16: "Another influence that drew me·to it ... a man serving two masters.").

The play can go as fast as the waiter can go. He detaches himself from the emotional upheavals of the other characters by moving backwards and forwards between the tables and takes the audience with him. In humming to himself, he demonstrates his emotional detachment from the behaviour of his guests and supplies the audience with a commentary on their actions and morals (Interview, pp. 15–16: "In order to avoid monotony ... serving two masters." and p. 20: "When the waiter ... you're telling the story").

Suggesting Further Activities

Which aspects of "confusion" does *Between Mouthfuls* illustrate?

Students should summarize the stages in the action and decide which "confusions" are present, e.g. confusion of meaning, situation, identity, understanding etc. Ayckbourn's own comments would be useful background information for the students (Interview, p. 17: "It's a word ... in themselves were an entity."). Their findings can then be compared with the use of "confusions" in the other two plays (Interview, p. 18: "I wanted to pursue ... totally different aspect.").

Assessment of the dramatic form

- In what way do the topics of the three plays lend themselves to an understanding of the characteristic features of the short play? (cp. p. 7)
- In what sense is the situation in *Between Mouthfuls* a critical situation? (cp. p. 7)

A Talk in the Park

A park

Four park benches, separated but not too distant from each other. On one sits Beryl, a belligerent young girl at present engrossed in reading a long letter. On another sits Charles who looks what he is, a businessman dressed for the weekend. He is slowly thumbing his way through a thick report. On another sits Doreen, middle-aged, untidily dressed, feeding the birds from a bag of breadcrumbs. On the remaining bench sits Ernest, a younger man. He sits gazing into space. The birds sing. After a moment, Arthur enters. He is a bird-like man in a long mackintosh, obviously on the look-out for company. Eventually, he approaches Beryl's bench

ARTHUR Is this seat occupied, by any chance?
BERYL *(shortly)* No. *(She continues to read)*
ARTHUR Great, great. *(He sits)*

A pause. Arthur takes deep breaths and gives a few furtive glances in Beryl's direction

Student, I see?
BERYL What?
ARTHUR Student, I bet. You look like a student. Always tell a student.
BERYL No.
ARTHUR Ah. You look like one. You're young enough to be a student. Quite young enough. That's the life, isn't it? Being a student. Not a care in the world. Sitting in the park on a day like this. In the sunshine. Rare enough we see the sun, eh? Eh? Rare.
BERYL Yes. *(She refuses to be drawn into conversation)*
ARTHUR Mind you, I shouldn't be here. By rights, I should be at home. That's where I should be. Inside my front door. I've got plenty of things I

---

belligerent [bɪ'lɪdʒərənt] aggressive
to be engrossed in [ɪn'grəʊst] to be concentrated on
to thumb one's way (through a book) to turn the pages, one after the other
mackintosh ['---] raincoat
furtive verstohlen
always tell a student I can always recognize a student
mind you you know

should be doing. The kitchen shelves to name but three. Only you sit at home on a day like today. Sunday. Nothing to do. On your own – you think to yourself, this is no good, this won't get things done – and there you are talking to yourself. You know what they say about people who talk to themselves? Eh? Eh? Yes. So I thought it's outdoors for you, else they'll come and take you away. Mind you, I'm never at a loss. I'm a very fulfilled person. I have, for example, one of the biggest collections of cigarette cards of anyone alive or dead that I know of. And you don't get that by sitting on your behind all day. But I'll let you into a secret. Do you know what it is that's the most valuable thing there is you can hope to collect? People. I'm a collector of people. I look at them, I observe them, I hear them talk, I listen to their manner of speaking and I think, hallo, here's another one. Different. Different again. Because I'll let you into a secret. They are like fingerprints. They are never quite the same. And I've met a number in my lifetime. Quite a number. Some good, some bad, all different. But the best of them, and I'm saying this to you quite frankly and openly, the best of them are women. They are superior people. They are better people. They are cleaner people. They are kinder-hearted people. If I had a choice, I'd be a woman. Now that makes you laugh, I expect, but it's the truth. When I choose to have a conversation, I can tell you it's with a woman every time. Because a woman is one of nature's listeners. Most men I wouldn't give the time of day to. Now I expect that shocks you but it's the truth. Trouble is, I don't get to meet as many women as I'd like to. My particular line of work does not bring me into contact with them as much as I would wish. Which is a pity.

Beryl gets up

BERYL Excuse me. *(She moves off)*

ARTHUR Are you going?

Beryl moves to Charles's bench

I'm never at a loss I can always find s.th. to do
cigarette card picture card (of sportsmen, film stars, etc.) included in a packet of cigarettes
(the) trouble is the difficulty is
my line of work the kind of work I do

BERYL *(to Charles)* Excuse me, is this seat taken?

CHARLES *(barely glancing up)* No. *(He moves along his bench)*

BERYL *(sitting)* Thanks. Sorry, only the man over there won't stop talking. I wanted to read this in peace. I couldn't concentrate. He just kept going on and on about his collections or something. I normally don't mind too much, only if you get a letter like this, you need all your concentration. You can't have people talking in your ear – especially when you're trying to decipher writing like this. He must have

---

to decipher writing [dɪ'saɪfə] to be able to read (bad) handwriting

been stoned out of his mind when he wrote it. It wouldn't be unusual. Look at it. He wants me to come back. Some hopes. To him. He's sorry, he didn't mean to do what he did, he won't do it again I promise, etc., etc. I seem to have heard that before. It's not the first time, I can tell you. And there's no excuse for it, is there? Violence. I mean, what am I supposed to do? Keep going back to that? Every time he loses his temper he ... I mean, there's no excuse. A fracture, you know. It was nearly a compound fracture. That's what they told me. *(Indicating her head)* Right here. You can practically see it to this day. Two X-rays. I said to him when I got home, I said, "You bastard, you know what you did to my head?" He just stands there. The way he does. "Sorry," he says, "I'm ever so sorry." I told him. I said, "You're a bastard, that's what you are. A right, uncontrolled, violent, bad-tempered bastard." You know what he said? He says, "You call me a bastard again and I'll smash your stupid face in." That's what he says. I mean, you can't have a rational, civilized discussion with a man like that, can you? He's a right bastard. My friend Jenny, she says, "You're a looney, leave him for God's sake. You're a looney." Who needs that? You tell me one person who needs that? Only where do you go? I mean, there's all my things – my personal things. All my – everything. He's even got my bloody Post Office book. I'll finish up back there, you wait and see. I must be out of my tiny mind. Eh. Sometimes I just want to jump down a deep hole and forget it. Only I know that bastard'll be waiting at the bottom. Waiting to thump the life out of me. Eh?

CHARLES Yes. Excuse me. *(He gets up)*

BERYL I'm sorry, I didn't mean to embarrass you.

CHARLES No, no.

---

stoned out of his mind *(sl.)* completely drugged or drunk
some hopes it will never happen
to lose one's temper to become angry
fracture broken bone
compound ['––] **fracture** fracture causing a skin wound
X-rays photographs made by the method discovered by Röntgen
to smash s.o.'s face in to hit s.o. hard in the face
looney *(sl.)* lunatic, crazy person
Post Office book savings-book into which one can pay money or draw it out at the post office
to thump the life out of s.o. *(colloq.)* to attack and hit s.o. again and again

BERYL I just had to ...

CHARLES Quite all right. Quite all right.

Charles moves over to Doreen

(To Doreen) Nobody here, is there?

DOREEN What?

CHARLES Nobody here?

DOREEN Nobody where? *(She looks round)*

CHARLES Sitting here.

DOREEN No. No.

CHARLES Sorry. Do you mind if I do? *(He sits)* I won't disturb you. Girl over there's got boy-friend trouble. Comes and pours it all out on me – as if I'm interested. I mean, we've all been through it at one time or another. Why should she think I should be interested. I mean, we've all got troubles no doubt. But we all don't sit on a bench and bore some poor innocent stranger to death. I mean, that in my book spells S for selfishness. And have you noticed that it's invariably the young? They think we haven't been through it. Can't imagine that perhaps we were young, too. Don't know where they think we all came from. I mean, five years ago I had a house in the country, a charming wife, two good children, couldn't imagine a happier family. My wife dies suddenly, my children can't stand the place a moment longer and emigrate to Canada so I sell the house and there I am in a flat I can hardly swing a cat in. But I don't go round boring other people with it. That's life. I've had twenty – no, more like twenty-five, good years. Who am I to complain if I get a few bad ones thrown in as well. Make no mistake, I know I'm in for some bad ones. Things are going to get worse before they get better. Bound to. And you know an interesting thing about trouble? I always think it's a bit like woodworm. Once

---

to bore s.o. to death jdn zu Tode langweilen
invariably [ɪnˈveərɪəblɪ] always
I can hardly swing a cat *(colloq.)* said of a room, flat, etc., which is much too small
I get bad ones thrown in as well I have to live through bad years as well as good ones
to be in for s.th. to expect s.th. bad or unpleasant
bound to it will surely happen
woodworm small insect which bores holes in wood

you've got a dose, if you're not careful, it starts to spread. Starts in your family and, before you know it, it's into your business. Which explains why I'm sitting here reading a report that's been put together so badly that I've got to read it through on my one day off and condense it into another report before I can even be certain whether I'm bankrupt. I mean, I don't know if you're interested but just take a look at this page here, this is a typical page. Can you make head or tail ...

Doreen gets up and moves away

(Muttering) Oh, I beg your pardon.

Doreen moves to Ernest's bench

DOREEN Excuse me.

ERNEST Eh?

DOREEN Excuse me. May I sit here for a moment? *(She sits)* The man over there has been – you know – I didn't want to make a scene but he – you know. I mean, I suppose I should call the police – but they'd never catch him. I mean, most of the police are men as well, aren't they? Between you and me, I have heard that most of the police women are as well. Men dressed up, you know. Special Duties, so called. So my ex-husband informed me. I mean, it's terrible, you can't sit in a park these days without some men – you know – I mean, I'm on a fixed income – I don't want all that. That comes from my husband. My ex-husband. He runs a pub. In the country. But I had to leave him. We got to the stage when it was either that or – you know. I love dogs, you see, but he would never – he refused, point blank. And the day came when I knew I must have a dog. It became – you know – like an obsession. So I left. I usually have my dog here with me only he's at the vet's. He's only a puppy. They had to keep him in.

---

dose [dəʊs] s.th. unpleasant; e.g. 'a dose of medicine'
can you make head or tail (of s.th.)? can you find any sense (in s.th.)?
dressed up verkleidet
special duties work on special cases, when the police do not wear uniforms
we got to the stage ... we reached the point ...
to refuse point blank to say no as a final answer
obsession s.th. that one thinks about all the time and cannot forget
vet *short for:* veterinary surgeon; animal doctor
puppy very young dog

He's being – you know – poor little thing. He'd have seen that man off. He's a loyal little dog. He understands every word I say to him. Every word. I said to him this morning, Ginger-boy, I said – you're coming down to the vet's with me this morning to be – you know, and his little ears pricked up and his tail wagged. He knew, you see. I think dogs are more intelligent than people. They're much better company and the wonderful thing is that once you've got a little dog, you meet other people with dogs. And what I always say is that people who have dogs they're the nicest sort of people. They're the ones I know I'd get on with.

Ernest gets up

Have you got a dog, by any chance?

Ernest ignores her and creeps behind the trees to Arthur

ERNEST *(sitting down next to Arthur)* Excuse me. Just taking refuge. Nut case over there. Bloody woman prattling on about her dog. Ought to be locked up. Thinks every man's after her. I mean, look. Look at it. After her? She'd have to pay 'em. You know the sort though, don't you? I mean, if you let her talk to you long enough, she'll talk herself into thinking you've assaulted her. Before you know it, she's screaming blue murder, you'll be carried off by the fuzz and that's your lot. Two years if you're lucky. I mean, I came out here just to get away from the wife. Don't want another one just like her, do I? I mean. That's why I'm in the park. Get away from the noise. You got kids? Don't have kids. Take my tip, don't get married. Well, looks all right, but believe me – nothing's your own. You've paid for it all but nothing's your own. Yap, yap, yap. Want, want, want. Never satisfied.

---

to see s.o. off *here:* to chase s.o. away
Ginger ['dʒɪndʒə] name for a dog (or s.o.) with red hair
his ears pricked up (of a dog) his ears stood up straight to show that he was interested
to wag to move to and fro
to take refuge ['refju:dʒ] to hide away from s.th. unpleasant
nut case *(sl.)* crazy person
to prattle to chatter, to talk in a childish, simple way
to assault [ə'sɔ:lt] to attack
to scream blue murder *(colloq.)* to shout very loudly when attacked
fuzz *(coll.)* police
to yap to bark like a small dog, to chatter in an irritating way

I mean, no word of a lie, I look at her some mornings and I think, blimey, I must have won last prize in a raffle. Mind you, I dare say she's thinking the same. In fact, I know she is. Certainly keeps me at a distance. Hallo, dear, put your money on the table and she's off out. Don't see her for dust. Sunday mornings, it's a race to see who can get out first. Loser keeps the baby. Well, this morning I made it first. Here I am in the quiet. Got away from the noise. You know something interesting? Most of our lives are noise, aren't they? Artificial man-made noise. But you sit out here and you can listen – and – well, there's a bit of traffic but apart from that – peace. Like my mother used to say. Shut your eyes in the country and you can hear God breathing. *(He shuts his eyes)*

ARTHUR *(leaning across to Beryl)* Hey – hey – pssst! I've got a right one here. Thinks he's listening to God breathing … *(He laughs)*

BERYL *(leaning across to Charles)* He's talking again. To me. What do you do? *(She smiles)*

CHARLES *(leaning across to Doreen)* There she goes again. What did I tell you? Chapter Two of the boyfriend saga.

DOREEN *(leaning across to Ernest)* He's talking to me. If he does it any more, I'll call the police …

ERNEST *(to Arthur)* Oh, blimey. Why doesn't she go home? Hark at her. Can you hear her? Rabbitting on …

The following, final section, is played as a Round. Doreen finishes first, then Charles cuts out, followed by Beryl, Arthur, and then Ernest

ARTHUR *(to Beryl)* Hey –hey …

Beryl continues to ignore him

Oh, suit yourself.

BERYL *(to Charles)* Psst – psst …

---

blimey ['blaɪmɪ] exclamation of surprise, irritation, etc. (from 'God blind me')
raffle lottery
don't see her for dust *(colloq.)* she goes so quickly that I hardly see her go
saga *here:* very long story
to hark at s.o. *(coll.)* to listen to s.o.
rabbitting on talking without stopping
round *(mus.)* canon for three or more voices, which start and finish at different times. 'Oh, wie wohl ist mir am Abend' is a round.

Charles ignores her

Oh, be like that.

CHARLES *(to Doreen)* I say, I say …

Doreen ignores him

Oh, all right, don't then …

DOREEN *(to Ernest)* Excuse me, excuse me, excuse me.

Ernest ignores her

Oh, really.

ERNEST *(nudging Arthur)* Oy – oy …

Arthur ignores him

Oh, all right, then. Don't. Don't then. Might as well talk to yourself.

They all sit sulkily. The Lights fade to a Black-out, and –

the CURTAIN *falls*

---

to nudge s.o. jdm einen leichten Stoß geben; ‚anschubsen'
sulky saying nothing because one is in a bad temper
to fade to become less bright

Introducing the Play

In a small park there are four benches, each occupied by a person. The occupants are strangers to each other. A man called Arthur (A) enters the park and sits down on the bench occupied by Beryl (B) who is reading. Arthur has fled from the loneliness of his home to seek company outdoors and tries to initiate a conversation with Beryl. Beryl refuses, however, to be drawn into conversation with the result that Arthur's talking evolves into a lengthy monologue in which he says that women generally are superior and better people, kinder and cleaner, and good listeners. He regrets very much that his work does not offer him a lot of opportunities to meet women. Obviously irritated at Arthur's intrusion Beryl gets up and moves over to the nearby bench where Charles (C) is sitting. The letter which she had been trying to read before Arthur encroached on her privacy is from her ex-boyfriend and the subject matter of her monologue in Charles' presence. But Beryl's troubles are not a source of interest to Charles who without commenting in the least gets up and moves over to the next bench where Doreen (D) is sitting. Charles in turn tells Doreen all the personal problems he has had since his wife died. Without showing any interest Doreen moves over to the next bench and for her part opens up her heart to Ernest (E) who is sitting there. Ignoring her question as to whether he had a dog, Ernest gets up and creeps behind the trees to where Arthur is sitting and tells him all his domestic troubles. Arthur doesn't reply to Ernest but tries to comment on him to Beryl who in turn directs her attention to Charles who then turns to Doreen and so on. At the end of the play Arthur says "Might as well talk to yourself".

Analysing the text

THEMES – STATEMENTS – QUESTIONS – QUOTATIONS

Suggestions and guidelines which can be used as starting points for classroom work and discussion. First numbers refer to the pages in the Students' Book, numbers in brackets refer to the lines.

Lack and loss of communication

- "Girl over there's got boy-friend trouble. Comes and pours it all out on me – as if I'm interested." ▷ 49 (10–12)

Discussion prompt:
Are the characters speaking to communicate, or to relieve their own feelings?

- "Might as well talk to yourself." ▷ 53 (11)

Discussion prompt:
Is there any communication between the characters?

- "I'm a very fulfilled person. I have, for example, one the biggest collections of cigarette cards of anyone alive or dead that I know of." ▷ 46 (7–9)

Discussion prompt:
Do the characters talk about anything of any real importance?

Aspects of isolation

- Arthur … is on his own – despite ingenious attempts to find an interest in life he remains isolated – he has developed a philosophy of life to compensate for this
- Beryl … is on her own – she has left her boy-friend but cannot find a replacement for her unsatisfactory relationship – isolated by fear and violence – defeatist philosophy
- Charles … is on his own – his wife is dead – what was a fulfilled life is now in ruins – tries to find a substitute fulfillment in his work – circumstances have forced him into isolation – forces himself to be philosophical
- Doreen … is on her own – she has divorced her husband – finds a substitute for human affection in her dog – deliberately isolates herself from people – has opted out of making sense of her life

– Ernest … is on his own – emotionally isolated from his family – yearns for peace and quiet – adopts his mother's philosophy

Discussion prompt:
Do the characters have anything in common?
Could Ayckbourn have given any character other than Arthur the bitterly ironic line, "I'm a very fulfilled person?"

Language and character

– Arthur	Standard, middle-class English. Short sentences piled upon one another:	
	"I look at them, I observe them, I hear them talk …"	▷ 46 (12)
	Standard phrases:	
	"My particular line of work."	▷ 46 (26)
	Expresses original ideas in poetic terms:	
	"They are like fingerprints."	▷ 46 (14)
	"A woman is one of nature's listeners."	▷ 46 (23)
– Beryl	Slightly northern, very working-class English. Use of direct speech Unsophisticated linguistic style Uncouth expressions: "stoned", "bastard", "I'll smash your stupid face in." – "You're a looney."	
– Charles	Standard, upper middle-class English. More polished, educated language. Middle-class allusions, e.g. "a house in the country." Structure of sentences more complex.	
– Doreen	Slightly Cockney, working-class English. Disjointed sentences which she	

	does not finish when the topic verges on sexuality: "He's being – you know – poor little thing."	▷ 51 (1)
	Avoids use of "rape" and "castrate" Allusions to sexual perversion.	
– Ernest	Stronger Cockney accent than Doreen, working-class.	
	Slovenly way of speaking: "Don't want another one just like her, do I? I mean."	▷ 51 (22)
	Speech interspersed with slang: "Nut case", "prattling", "screaming blue murder", "the fuzz", "kids". Allusions to betting:	
	"I must have won last prize in a raffle."	▷ 52 (2)
	"Loser keeps the baby."	▷ 52 (6)

Discussion prompt:
Does the way the characters express themselves give any insight into their lives, social backgrounds and personalities?

Telling details

– Arthur	"One of the biggest collections of cigarette cards."	▷ 46 (7–8)
– Beryl	"He's even got my bloody Post Office book."	▷ 48 (21)
– Charles	"A house in the country, a charming wife, two good children."	▷ 49 (19–20)
– Doreen	"My ex-husband", "a fixed income", "He runs a pub."	▷ 50
– Ernest	"Put your money on the table." (weekly pay-packet)	▷ 52 (4)

Discussion prompt:
Each character talks about subjects with which he or she is preoccupied. The details they include give us more background information and help towards a fuller understanding of the characters and the backgrounds they come from. Describe how you picture the five characters on stage.

Monologues or soliloquies?

– "Might as well talk to yourself." ▷ 53 (11)

Discussion prompt:
The play consists of a series of monologues which could equally well be termed soliloquies for all the notice taken of them. Would it make any difference to a) the characters, b) the audience if there were only one character on the stage at any one time?

The women versus the men and vice versa

– "... the best of them are women. They are superior people. They are better people." ▷ 46 (18–19)
– "I look at her some mornings and I think, blimey, I must have won last prize in a raffle." ▷ 52 (1–2)

Discussion prompt:
Each character gives, or implies, an opinion on the relationships between man and woman, husband and wife. Which opinions are voiced in *A Talk in the Park*? Are similar ideas expressed in any of the other plays?

Kafka and the alphabet

"... the best way to describe it is that it is an inevitable play ... the characters are labelled A, B, C, D, E, although they have all got names ... You're into very strange Kafka territory ..." (Interview, p. 17).

Discussion prompt:
The structure and development of the play are predictable from the beginning. Ayckbourn meant it to be so. How do the characters maintain the audience's interest? Is the end of the play entirely predictable?

Presenting the Cassette

Predicting the dialogue and action

The play is the most reflective of the three. It has fewer devices for provoking laughter or arousing suspense. It might, therefore, be necessary to create interest in advance and a willingness to listen carefully. Groups of students could be given the stage directions at the beginning of the play (Students' Book, p. 45). This would give them a sketch of each character. Each group must choose a character and try to predict what their character will talk about and do. The results can be discussed and then compared with the Cassette; each speech being dealt with individually.

The round at the end of the play

The round is a difficult piece of stage business to visualize. Students could attempt to read this last part of the scene themselves and compare their ideas with the version on the Cassette.

Producing the Play

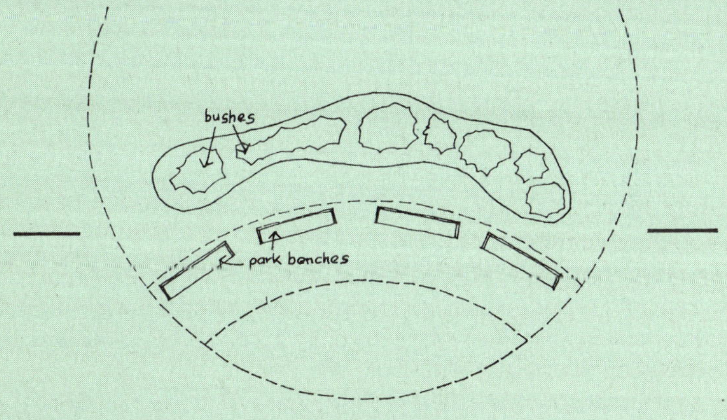

A Talk in the Park

On stage: *4 park benches*
Bushes

Personal: **Beryl:** 3-page letter
Arthur: old brown carrier-bag
Charles: brown folder with report
Doreen: old handbag, bag of breadcrumbs, spectacles, dog-lead in pocket

(*Confusions*. London: French 1977, p. 64)

Which costumes would be appropriate for which characters?

Costumes are more important in this play than in the other two. The park is a neutral meeting place, so the audience has to rely on what people say and what they look like. Invite students to use the hints given in the dialogue to suggest appropriate costumes.

Are the stage properties essential?

Pupils could discuss whether the stage properties, e.g. 3-page letter, could be dispensed with by using mime, or whether, in a low budget production, the costumes could more easily be dispensed with in favour of jeans and T-shirts.

Discussing the Interview

Dialogue and character study

The play presents the audience with a selection of very different social types. The setting is neutral, unlike the middle-class restaurant in *Between Mouthfuls*, which indicates to the audience what kind of characters to expect. We have to judge by appearances, as we would if observing this scene in a real park. The introductory stage directions give some indication, but there are also clues to the social standing of the characters in the dialogue, e.g. Beryl's Post Office Book (Details: Interview, pp. 21–22: "I don't know ... all sorts of references."). Students could make lists of these references and write a description of the characters according to their findings.

How does the structure of *A Talk in the Park* differ from the other two plays?

The first two plays begin in a naturalistic way and work up through varying degrees of farce to an unexpected climax. An element of curiosity, if not quite suspense, keeps the audience guessing up to the very last moment. *A Talk in the Park,* on the other hand, is predictable in its outcome. The pattern is set from the beginning: a circle, not an upward curve (Interview, p. 17: "In a strange way ... you expect the chord and it happens.").

Suggesting Further Activities

Observation as a basis for character study

"Arthur gets very near being the writer in his thing about people and observing them." (Interview, p. 21)

This, or Ayckbourn's comments that Lucy in *Mother Figure* was based on his wife, might be a good starting-point for encouraging students to attempt a little play-writing of their own. They have almost certainly observed that members of their family or friends or neighbours have pet subjects which they can always talk about in predictable ways. Using this as a basis, they could try to construct a short "park bench soliloquy" for them – along the lines of Ayckbourn's characters.

Alternatively, students could choose some well-known personality instead of someone from their immediate family or friends.

Comparison of the play with Edward Albee's *The Zoo Story*

A Talk in the Park could be read with students before or after a discussion of Edward Albee's *The Zoo Story.* The setting of *The Zoo Story* is also a park. There are two benches comparable to the four park benches in *A Talk in the Park.* Peter and Jerry, the two characters in this short play, "start off as strangers. But Albee's dialogue convinces us that within the short time (less than an hour) that the play runs, Jerry inflicts himself on Peter with such uncompromising determination that in spite of all Peter's efforts to fend him off, he gets to know Jerry better than he has ever known his wife or his daughters and better than he will ever get to know anyone else. In fact he will be lonelier than before, because more aware of his aloneness" (Ronald Hayman, *Edward Albee.* Contemporary Playwrights Series, London: Heinemann 1971, p. 1).

Assessment of the dramatic form

What are the character traits that the portrayal of the five characters in *A Talk in the Park* has been reduced to? (cf. One-Act and Short Play, p. 7)

What does the performance of the three plays during one evening require of the audience? (Students' Book, p. 6)

Blackboard:

If the three diagrams represent the acting of the three one-act plays in this collection, which diagram is most appropriate to which play?

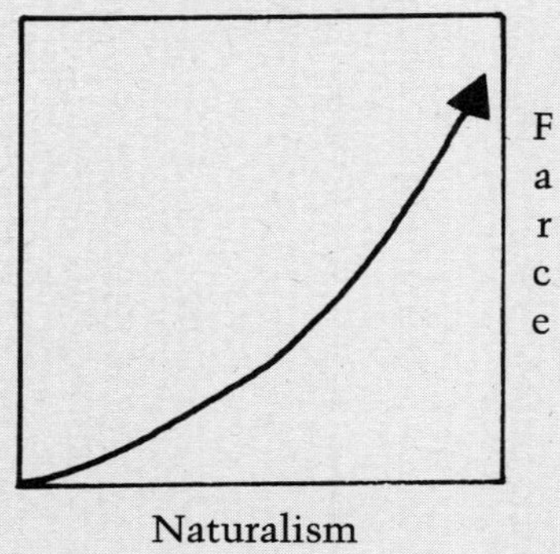

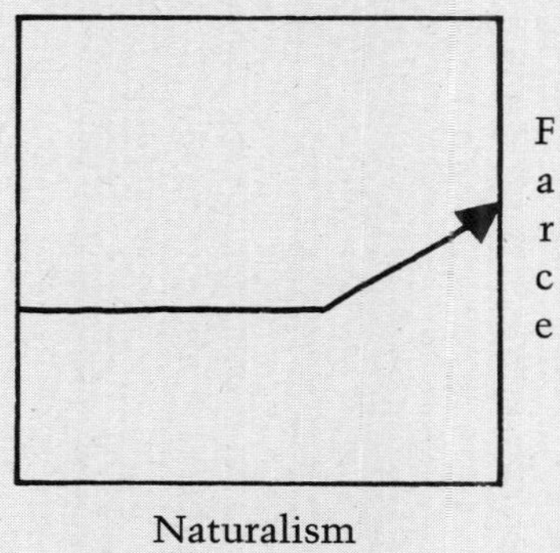

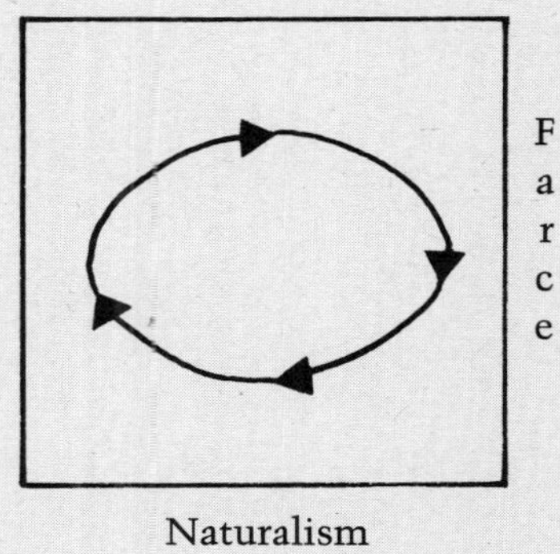

Mother Figure
Gradual movement from naturalistic presentation into farce. Unexpected ending.

Between Mouthfuls
Naturalistic, mixed with farce until near end, then slightly more rapid movement into area of farce. Unexpected ending.

A Talk in the Park
Circular movement. Predictable ending.

Select Bibliography

1. Reference Books

Abrams, M. H. *A Glossary of Literary Terms.* (3rd ed.) New York 1971.

Bodenschatz, Herbert. *Englisches Lernwörterbuch zur Textanalyse.* Frankfurt/M. 1979

Scott, A. F. *Current Literary Terms. A Concise Dictionary of their Origin and Use.* London 1967.

Werlich, Egon. *Wörterbuch der Textinterpretation. The Field System Dictionary for Text Analysis.* (8th print.) Dortmund 1978.

2. Contemporary English Drama

Glaap, Albert-Reiner. *Das englische Drama seit 1970. Hintergrundinformationen und Unterrichtsvorschläge für die Sekundarstufe II.* Limburg 1979.

Groene, Horst/Schik, Berthold, eds. *Das moderne Drama im Englischunterricht der Sekundarstufe II. Grundlegungen – Interpretationen – Kursprojekte.* Königstein/Ts. 1980

Hayman, Ronald. *British Theatre since 1955. A Reassessment.* Oxford 1979.

Kerensky, Oleg. *The New British Drama. Fourteen Playwrights since Osborne and Pinter.* London 1977.

Kosok, Heinz, ed. *Drama und Theater im England des 20. Jahrhunderts.* Düsseldorf 1980.

„Lektüre zeitgenössischer Dramen." *Der fremdsprachliche Unterricht* 62 (1982).

„Modernes englisches Drama." *anglistik & englischunterricht* 7 (1979).

Taylor, John Russell. *The Second Wave. British Drama for the Seventies.* London 1971.

Weber, Hans, ed. *Dramen des 20. Jahrhunderts für den Englischunterricht in der Sekundarstufe II.* Frankfurt 1982.